The Conflict of Indian Press

Deveriya Unmesh

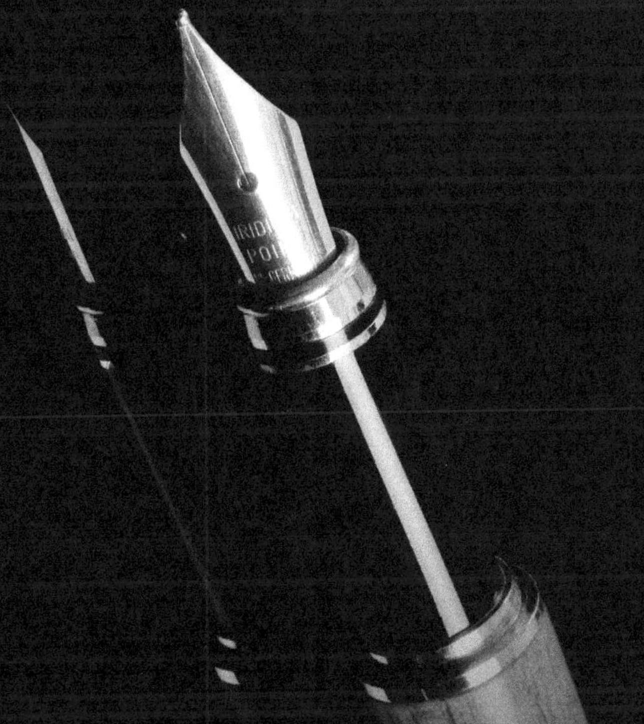

The Conflict Of Indian Press

Deveriya Unmesh

THE CONFLICT OF INDIAN PRESS

First published in 2008

Printed at and published by Rashid Khosravi for Media Research Centre (proposed),
B-1/17 Moraya Residency-I, Sus Road, Pune (India)-411021

ISBN: 9798542526485

Legal disputes within the municipal limits of Pune city only.

Acknowledgements

I take this opportunity to record my special thanks to Mr. Nicholas Coleridge whose work, 'The Paper Tigers' inspired me to attempt a separate volume on the modus operandi and accolades of a section of Indian press barons. Thanks are due mainly to Mr. Madhu Shetye of the Bombay Press Club, Mr. Kolpe of the undivided Indian Express Group, advocate Manohar Dalal of Indore and the late Mr. Behram Contractor (of Busy-bee fame) for the invaluable information and the 'experienced truth' that they shared with me.

I am also thankful to Mr. Abhay Chhajalani of Nai Dunia whose almost photogenic presence on the pages of his own journal was a constant reminder to expedite the publication that you are holding. It would be sheer injustice, if I do not thank Mr. Suresh Seth (the ex-Mayor of Indore) whose virtual 'eclipse' on the political horizon of Madhya Pradesh enabled me to visualize the nexus between pulp whores and their power pimps. Besides, I am also thankful to Mr. Vijaya Datta Shridhar and Dr. Mangla Anuja of Madhav Rao Sapre Newspaper Museum (Bhopal) whose staff left no stone un-turned to help me with the past issues of requisite journals and publications. At length, I would like to thank advocate Rashid Khosravi without whose active involvement this volume would not have seen the light of day.

May their tribe increase!

Deveriya Unmesh

Dedication

This book is a tribute to late
Rahul Barpute
who initiated me in journalism
and whose chosen disciples caused mutation
in the genetically defunct manifestation of
Hindi journalism.

Table Of Content

Introduction

Chapter 1. The Psychology of Journalism
Whether media enterprise is really a service to the society, nation and Mankind or is it a "will to power" deep rooted in an ailment called 'Inferiority Complex' that eventually culminates into Megalomania? [First published in Bhavan's Journal dated December15, 2006].

Chapter 2. The Philosophy of Propaganda
Whether Journalism has lost its missionary zeal to inform and educate people and has been reduced to a device of propaganda aimed at manufacturing consent as observed by Noam Chomsky? Illustrated with the help of examples from USA and India [First published in Bhavan's Journal dated May15, 2007].

Chapter 3. The Indianization of the Times of India
How the British legacy was first Indianized by R. K. Dalmia and then by his son-in-law; a continuous process of change initiated by Mr. Sameer Jain.

Chapter 4. The Indian Express: Myth and Reality
A brief history of the journal; what Mr. Dom Moraes learnt from Seth Goenka; the observations of Bhabtosh Dutta Committee and other govt. agencies about this journal; Goenka as an employer; the beneficiaries of Goenka's split vision.

Chapter 5. The Mecca of Hindi Journalism
The strategic importance of Indore in the opium related parlance; the prevailing nexus and its modus operandi;

Marg in New Delhi. A comparative review of the TOI, DNA, Indian Express and the Bombay edition of HT.

Chapter 11. The Emerging Scenario
The decline of qualitative journalism in India and the circulation figures in USA.The advent of electronic media; the mushroom growth of tabloids and broadsheets in the Hindi Heartland; the tendency to monopolize in the garb of multi-edition ventures; a list of multi-edition dailies and single editions with more than one lakh circulation.

Chapter 12. Addressed to the Editor
An attempt to categorize editors as per their attitudes /aptitudes and psychological constraints. The observations of Mr. Vinod Mehta. Corporate communication and the print media- observations of late Chanchal Sarkar. The power-drunk who does not respond to communications. Mr. Ravindra Kumar's observations about circulation figures. The dichotomy of media's gender.

Prologue

Before the advent of journalism
the arch angel ran an ad-agency
That separated truth from those
Who worshipped forms and icons.

It was Adam who rescued
devil from God, evolution
from the Buddha, and
Narcissus, from andropause.

It was I, who suffered from
Prophetic illusions, rescued
Nietzsche, from sanity;
Lunatics, from editing.

Once again, I may rescue
The embryonic Phoenix
from the exhibitionists.
And the rest is journalism.

1. The Psychology Of Journalism[1]

Given a choice between megalomania and narcissism, no sane person would like to opt for either. But the majority of our press barons have not only mistaken their ailment for the term, "media enterprise" but have also conditioned their editors to believe them. Wherever there was a little scope for sanity, the same was aborted by a hybrid species called, "proprietor-editor" for which the current coinage is "aboriginal editor". Nietzsche has summarized the implied ailment as "will to power". According to him, "There is in fact no alternative to gods; either they are the will to power-and so long as they are that they will be national gods-or else the impotence for power-and then they necessarily become good". (Quoted from Nietzsche's seminal work, Anti- Christ). What Nietzsche had described as "will to power" was subsequently described as "inferiority complex" by Alfred Adler.

Borrowing the gist from Nietzsche's concept of megalomania (without acknowledging it, of course) Salman Rushdie has raised two questions in Satanic Verses: what is

---

[1] First published in the Bhavan's Journals dated December 15, 2006

one's ideology and to what extent one compromises with it when he or she is the weakest. The second question is an Alexandrian one through which he asks: how do you behave with your enemies when they have already surrendered to you. In the light of Nietzsche's analysis and Rushdie's solitude, every press baron in India is confronted with two questions: whether he knows the difference between megalomania and business enterprise and if so, how does he behave with a smuggler- turned builder-turned - press baron-turned politician? Similarly, every politician should also be asked if he is aware of the difference between megalomania and "democratic participation in the executive wing of the Government" and if so, how does he behave with the press baron who is eating in to the vitals of democracy by extending patronage to the nexus between the criminal and the politician on the one hand and between the press and the politician on the other.

In a different context, every press baron in India is also confronted with an additional set of two questions: (i) whether he knows the difference between ambition and megalomania and if yes, how does he behave with those members of his editorial staff who are already aware of such a difference? Similarly, every journalist who claims to be objective in his approach is required to answer the following two questions:

i) is he aware that journalists are invariably governed by predatory forces which in turn, are governed by power maniacs;

ii) if yes, then how does he reconcile his sanity while working for a maniac?

There are exceptions in both the situations which only prove the generality of the dichotomy. As regards the journalist, the only exception is one working for a political ideology or an embassy where he has mistaken his subjective devotion for an objective illusion due mainly to the jargon implied in the ideology. Likewise, there can be another set of dichotomy for the Chief Editor or the Editorial Director:

   (i) does he know the difference between mediocrity and excellence with respect to himself;

   (ii) if yes, how does he behave with those of his editorial colleagues whose presence may arouse a sense of inferiority in him and may eclipse his status as their leader.

However, the above sets of dichotomies are not a prelude to the academic debate on editor's freedom or its dilution but a sincere attempt to psychoanalyze the behaviour pattern of those who are considered opinon leaders in Democracy. The ownership of mass-media for a covert criminal is perhaps as indispensable as the patronage of a commercial bank to an ambitious industrialist and that of a library to an intellectual. Journalism, which was a mission in the pre-independence era, has now emerged as 'journacracy' with remote control at the hands of 'journacrat' who never desists from masquerading as a "kingmaker" for politicians while himself remaining an object of case study for the psychiatrist. Needless to say, exceptions are always there. At this point, it would be interesting to compare two different attitudes regarding the press as experienced by the first prime minister of independent India and the first press baron who took over from the British. Jawaharlal Nehru wanted the Indian press to enjoy freedom, both from Government control and manipulation by money power. Therefore, he favoured a completely free press with all the dangers involved in the wrong use of that freedom than a surrendered or regulated press. For Nehru the term "freedom of press" was not restricted to interference by the government only as he had once clarified, "freedom of the press usually means non-interference by government but there is such a thing as interference by private interests. I am unable to understand how a small group represents the freedom of the press. The act of a big industry by itself owning a news paper and owning chains of newspapers cannot be said to give the press the kind of freedom which the public should expect of it.[2]

What Nehru had hinted as "interference by private interests" manifested itself during 1950's in the form of widespread allegations that PTI did not cover certain events which could adversely affect the business interests of Ramkrisna Dalmia. According to Mr. GNS Raghavan, the proceedings of Dalmia's trial at the Delhi Sessions Court were reported by Mr. A. Balu. One day, Mr. Dalmia complained to him that the reporting was unfair to him. Mr. Balu asked him to takeup the matter with the Delhi based Manager of PTI. The rest is a historical stricture against PTI. The First Press Commission condemned the Agency as a service of distrust as it was owned by the same publishers who owned the newspapers. The Commission also recommended the transfer of PTI to a public corporation by Parliament on the following grounds:

"It is clear to us that the present Board of Directors have no well formulated plan for meeting the growing demands which are made on the service and that if the present state

____

[2] PTI Story, Origin & Growth of the Indian Press and the News Agency' by GNS Raghavan, page 141

of affairs is allowed to continue, the Press Trust of India would continue to drift in uncertainty. We do not propose to deal in detail with the allegations of improper management and nepotism that have been brought to our notice or elaborate on complaints that have been made by witnesses that where certain business interests are concerned, The Press Trust of India has shown willingness to accommodate them by not covering news which might affect them adversely, and that in some cases PTI has gone out of its way to cover news which might publicise certain private interests... We are convinced that in the present international and national circumstances the news agency should work at the maximum of efficiency and integrity and for this purpose we recommend the setting up of a public corporation to take over the running of the Press Trust of India."[3]

Media pundits in India were convinced even before the globalization of the economy that newspaper is a consumer product and that he who pays the piper has the right to order the tune. This also resulted in vicarious liability when Mr. Pritish Nandy played a different tune in the editorial premises of the Illustrated Weekly of India. The dichotomy of the Indian press is deep rooted in public amnesia necessitating a flashback:

Scene I: The press baron returns after serving a prison term and asks his son-in-law to return or sell back the press that was sold or gifted to him. "Will you ask me to return your daughter also?" said the son-in-law. The rest is history.

Scene II: A budding enterpriser cum politician who worked as a broker at the Stock Exchange, was allegedly favoured with a pre-budget leak that metamorphosed bears

---

[3]Report of the Press Commission, Government of India, 1954 para 412

into bulls. The rest is the history created with the help of iron and steel.

Scene III: An enterprising editor of pauper Brahminical origin used to borrow money from the usufruct sharks in order to meet the running expenses of the press. On one occasion he failed to honour the pro-note. A money launderer turned builder turned industrialist emerged out of oblivion; honoured the blank pro-note (without lender's name); asked all concerned to sign the dotted line and grabbed the press against assets and liablilities. The rest of history is mafia friendly.

Scene IV: A tabloid published a story regarding the alleged love affair of Prime Minister's daughter who was already married. When the Prime Minister fired the editor, he explained his financial problems. Grapevine has it that the Prime Minister obliged him with cash.

Speaking at the All India Newspaper Editor's Conference in New Delhi on 17th September 1952 Jawaharlal Nehru had observed, "Does the freedom of the press ultimately mean freedom of the rich man to do what he likes with his money through the press? A poor man or a man with inadequate means whether he is good or bad, won't have much of an opportunity to express himself except in a very limited and small way. He may be good; he may be brilliant but the person who gets the opportunity now-a-days is the person with means; he can run newspapers, buy them or stop them, employ people whom he likes and dismiss people whom he dislikes. A great newspaper, while it is a very powerful organ, is at the same time a very expensive undertaking financially. Normally speaking--and I speak with all deference-- high standards and high intelligence are not allied with large quantity of money. A person with large amount

of money need not necessarily have high standards at all,
though he may have the knack of making money."
   Mr. aboriginal editor! are you listening?

2 The Philosophy Of Propaganda[4]

Walter Lippmann has opined that propaganda is "manufacture of consent."

Edward S. Herman and Noam Chomsky in their seminal work entitled, Manufacturing Consent, have observed, "Leaders of the media claim that their news choices rest on un-biased professional and objective criteria and they have support for this contention in the intellectual community. If, however, the powerful are able to fix the premises of discourse to decide what the general populace is allowed to see, hear and think about, and to "manage" public opinion by regular propaganda campaigns, the standard view of how the system works is at serious odds with reality."

Although propaganda may not constitute the total contents of a newspaper, it continues to be a very important aspect of their overall service. The propaganda model elaborated by them describes the forces that cause the media to play a propaganda role, the process whereby they mobilize bias and the patterns of news choice that ensue. Besides, they have demonstrated the applicability of the propaganda model to the actual performance of the media.

---

[4] First published in the Bhavan's Journal dated May 15, 2007

Their model traces the routes by which money and power are able to filter out the news fit to print, marginalize dissent and allow the government and dominant private interests to get their message across to the public. The dilution of propaganda into "news" takes place through various stages. These stages have been named as "filters" by the duo. The step-by-step filters are as follows:
   (i) The size, concentrated ownership, owner's wealth, and profit orientation of the dominant mass media;
   (ii) advertising as the primary income source of the Mass media;
   (iii)the reliance of the media on information provided by government, business "experts" funded and approved by these primary sources and agents of power;
   (iv)"flak" as a means of disciplining the media (refers to negative responses to a media statement or programme. It includes a letter of protest, a threat, a proposed legislation, law suit or punitive action.); and
   (v) "anti-Communism" as a notional religion and control mechanism.

While the last filter was more relevant to the USA before the collapse of the USSR, the relevance and the universality of the remaining four can hardly be over emphasized in any democratic set-up. The authors have also discussed the dichotomization of the propaganda campaigns with special reference to American foreign policy. For example, the torture of political prisoners and the attack on trade unions in Turkey was raised in the media only by human-rights activists while the US government supported the Turkish martial law government since its inception in 1980. In sharp contrast to this, the violations of the rights of trade unions in Poland was seen by the Reagan administration as a noble cause. Official sources in Washington were all set to distribute detailed hand-outs on human rights violations in Poland. Thus, apparently, there is dichotomization due to the filters but the result is the same: concentrate on the victims of enemy powers and forget about the victims of friends. As an example, they have quoted the following instance:

"the news of shooting down of the Korean airliner, KAL007 in 1983 was utilized by the US propaganda machinery as an outcry against the USSR throughout the world. But shooting down by Israel of a Libyan civilian airliner in 1973 raised no alarm. On the contrary, The New York Times had the audacity to highlight, "No useful purpose is served by an acrimonious debate over the assignment of blame for the downing of a Libyan airliner in the Sinai Peninsula last week[5]. Here the truth remains that the Soviets apparently did not know that they were shooting down a civilian plane. This was suppressed by the US officials. On the other hand, the Israelis were aware that they were shooting down a civilian plane.

Propaganda campaigns may be initiated either by the government or by the press baron. The campaign to discredit the government of Nicargua, to support the Salvadoran elections as an exercise in legitimizing democracy and to use the Soviet shooting down of the Korean airliner KAL007 as a means of mobilizing public support for the arms build-up were initiated by the government. The campaigns to publicize the crimes of Pol Pot and the alleged KGB plot to assassinate the Pope were initiated by the Readers Digest with strong follow-up support from NBC TV, The New York Times and other major media companies.

----

[5] Editorial, March 01, 1973

Some propaganda campaigns are jointly initiated by government and media; all of them require the collaboration of the mass-media. The government sponsored propaganda usually begins with a series of leaks by "a spokesman" or "reliable sources" at the press conference or through a press release. As against this, the media sponsored propaganda may begin with an article on the edit-page or a news item with a sign of interrogation or a letter to the editor or a statement in the name of a student leader who simply signs the text prepared by a sub-editor, who in turn, is directed by the press baron through proper channels. If the other newspapers like the story, they will follow it up, thus the matter becomes newsworthy. If there is no criticism or counter attack from any corner, the propaganda item becomes true even without any real evidence. Herman and Chomsky have quoted the following instances where propaganda was projected as news in the USA:

I. The KGB-Bulgarian plot to kill Pope: Free Market disinformation as "news".

II. Mass-media coverage of worthy and unworthy victims:
    (i) A murdered Polish priest versus one Hundred Murdered in Latin America;
    (ii) A murdered Polish priest versus two murdered officials of the Guatemalan mutual support group.

III. The savageries inflicted on worthy and unworthy victims, as depicted in New-York Times.

IV. Topics included and excluded in the New York Times' coverage of the Salvadoran Elections of March 25, 1984.

V. Topics included and excluded in the New York Times' coverage of the Nicarguan Elections planned for November 4, 1984.

The Indian Scenario

Perhaps it was C.P.Scott, the editor of Manchester Guardian who coined the phrase, "Fact are sacred, comment is free." In the Indian context, both are partly sacred and partly free depending upon the anticipated outcome of the "withheld news" as illustrated in the following example:

According to the Week (published from Cochi, India, September 27, 1998 issue), when the Narsimha Rao government decided to appoint M.K.Bezbaruah the Enforcement Director in 1995, an IAS colleague had asked him if he had met the Prime Minister. "Why should I "asked Bezbaruah slightly perplexed. The friend, who knew the poer corridors of New Delhi better, said, "If you don't go you will be called. "Bezbaruah replied that he would never go to the Prime Minister for advice on what he should or should not do. One of his orders on the taking-over was not to send the hawala case file to the Prime Minister or the Finance Minister for information. Three Prime Ministers succeeded Rao but Bezbaruah never went to any one of them." That is partly" says The Week, "why he recently lost the office and got it back-and is poised to lose it again." The Bezbaruah team had stalked Mr. Ashok Jain, the then Chairman of the Times of India group." The original whistle-blower was N.S.Hoon of Calcutta, a former business partner who fought Jain in the courts in Calcutta and Delhi for over a decade. Bezbaruah was convinced that Jain had committed serious FERA violations and ordered his custodial interrogation.

When the Finance Ministry directed him in 1996 not to arrest Jain and instead allow him to go to America for cardiac treatment, Bezbaruah insisted that Jain should be jailed when he returned. Jain's critics alleged that the Gujral and Vajpeyee regimes had shielded the media baron. Finally, the Directorate could interrogate Jain, though in hospital. The fallout was a massive media campaign that the Directorate was an anti-human rights fiend and that Bezbaruah and his men did not care for human dignity" (ibid).

In the beginning of 1977 an Enforcement Directorate raid on the New Delhi residence of the media baron was aborted mid-way following the personal intervention of the Revenue Secretary, N.K.Singh. According to a Bombay based tabloid,[6]" so incensed was Singh with M.K.Bezbaruah, that he immediately initiated a move for his punitive transfer. The transfer was stayed when the Supreme Court moved in the matter. Singh meanwhile, sought to explain this by asserting that both the then Prime Minister, Deve Gowda and the (then) Congress President, Sitaram Kesri had reprimanded him that night for having allowed the FERA raids on the media baron and wanted the same called off immediately." Curiously, the media baron approached the Delhi High Court against the FERA Directorate claiming that the raid on his house was malafide. A two-member bench of the Delhi High Court admitted the petition for hearing which effectively meant that the Directorate was not allowed to follow-up the case against the media baron till the Court finally disposed it off. "The petition follows the Enforcement Directorate's raid and subsequent detention of two Calcutta based businessmen who had allegedly transacted the 'hawala' deal with the media baron. It seems one of the raided businessmen had given Rs.17 crore worth of Foreign Exchange to the media baron abroad against the payment of an equivalent amount in Rupees in India. While the media baron could be relied upon to do all in his power

---

[6] The Afternoon Despatch and Courier dated 16.03.1997(Mumbai)

to get the investigation off his back, the most curious part is the gag order clamped on the press by the Delhi High Court. Even the former Prime Minister Narsimha Rao was not accorded the privilege of a gag order against the press while he faced his traducers like Lakhubhai Pathak and others in various courts.

"A couple of years ago when the FERA case against him first hit the headlines, the same media baron had secured a blanket gag order against the Bombay-based Free Press Journal group of newspapers. The presumptive censorship order against the FJP is still in place[7] despite attempts by the paper to have it withdrawn."

The background of controversy

According to newspaper reports the Enforcement Directorate had two strong clues to the charges of FERA violations by Mr. Ashok Jain. These clues necessitated thorough investigations abroad for which the Government of India's permission had already become overdue. The first clue was the bank guarantee of Rs.10 crore 80 lakh given by a bank in Zurich in 1985 on behalf of Mr. Ashok Jain. This let to a further link that Ashok Jain had an account in a foreign bank without permission of the Government of India. The Second clue is rooted in a statement given by Mr. Keshava Bangur to the officers of Enforcement Directorate to the effect that he had purchased the shares of the Bank of Rajasthan from Mr. Ashok Jain for which he had paid Rs.4 crore. It is alleged that this amount was deposited by Mr. Ashok Jain in his foreign account leading to interrogation of Mr. Prakash Khetan, a Calcutta based broker. It was gath-

---

[7] The date of this item in ADC is 16.03.97

ered that Mr. Ashok Jain had accounts in United Bank of Switzerland and American Express Bank.

The Kesri Factor

As regards the charges against Mr. Sitaram Kesri, it was gathered that he had opened an account with £ ten thousand at the Barclays Bank of London. This amount is alleged to have been provided by Mr. Alok Jain, who happens to be the brother of Mr. Ashok Jain. It is also alleged that one Mr. S.Hoon facilitated the opening of Mr. Kesri's account. This was further corroborated by Mr. Nirmal Kumar Jain, Secretary to Mr. Ashok Jain who stated that Mr. Kesri was present in London during 1969 and that he had stayed with Mr. Alok Jain at the Hilton Hotel. The investigating officials had also addressed certain enquiries to Mr. N.S.Hoon whose replies further focused the limelight (!) on both Mr. Ashok Jain and Mr. Sitaram Kesri. In one of the startling revelations Mr. Hoon alleged that Mr. Jain escaped charges under FERA during 1986 also when Mr. Bhurelal was Enforcement Director in the Rajiv Gandhi Regime. The matter was hushed-up for astronomical sums involving Mr. Ashok Jain and Mr. Sitaram Kesri for the second time. According to the Bombay edition of Jansatta dated 8th of June 1997 this "hush-up money" amounted to one hundred fifty crores of rupees (repeat, ONE HUNDRED FIFTY CRORES OF RUPEES)

The Prime Minister's media connection

Very few newspapers in the country were bold enough to publish the (then) Prime Minister's media connection when the media baron's New Delhi residence was raided by the Enforcement Directorate. Mr. I.K.Gujral was the Prime Minister at that time. According to certain exclusive reports, Gujral's sister's son, Amit Judge had married Nandita Jain, the daughter of Mr. Ashok Jain. Amit, once the owner of Stencil brand of shirts, subsequently joined the business empire of his in-laws. Jain's second son, Vineet is married to Amit Judge's sister. In all fairness to journalistic ethics, the same exclusive report also added, "Gujral, mindful of his image is unlikely of much help to Jain in cases where there existed clinching evidence against the latter."8

According to reports published in a section of the press on 8th and 9th of June 1997, a team of Information Bureau (IB) had questioned certain officers of the Enforcement Directorate as to how the news of the alleged involvement of Sitaram Kesri and Ashok Jain in the violation of FERA was leaked by two newspapers. In the background lies the news report published in The Stateman that highlighted the correspondence between the Ministry of Finance and Enforcement Direcotrate and another news item published in The Hindu which revealed the seven questions addressed to one Mr. S.Hoon of Canada by the Enforcement Directorate. The most glaring question was whether the addressee had paid any amount to Mr. Sitaram Kesri for opening a bank account abroad.

The fact remains that during those days bail under FERA cases was an exception rather than a norm and the suspects had to remain in the interrogation chambers of the ED for a custodial interrogation. Before targeting Ashok Jain, Mr. Bezbaruah had already interrogated corporate icons like ITC triumvirate of YC.Deveshwar, K.L.Chugh and

---

8 Afternoon on Sunday (Mumbai, 27-04-1997)

J.N.Sapru. Those suspicious of of their turn had already made Mr. Bezbaruah controversial in the media. The TOI had given full coverage to the event on the front page highlighting the reaction of Mr. Ashok Jain and that of the FICCI Chairman against the interrogation of corporate icons facing criminal charges under FERA. However, the million dollar question which remained unpublished, unanswered and unheard is the mental state of the five star editor who perhaps never felt embarrassed as an employee of the accused, facing criminal charges. Once the word "criminal" is prefixed, it is hardly material whether the charges are under FERA or IPC or Cr.P.C. It is in this context that every self respecting editor should ask himself the following questions:

I.   Would he relinquish his position if the charges against his employer are eventually proved. If not, would he opt for a better job in the underworld empire of a mafia don who has a potential to emerge as a press baron in due course ?

II. If his employer asks him to launch a media campaign against the interrogation of accused persons as a violation of human rights, would he do so for the cause of all those who are being interrogated for criminal charges such as dacoity, murder, rape, espionage till their respective charges are proved ?

III. Is he aware of the foundation of Natural Justice, and if so, can his employer be a judge in his own case. If not, how would he justify the sermons against injustice in his own newspaper or about objective reporting to his own juniors ?

Unfortunately, the editor concerned failed to rise to the occasion at 7 Bahadur Shah Zafar Marg. What is more alarming to note is the fact that the TOI happens to be the first Indian newspaper that had appointed a retired Supreme Court Judge as its Press Ombudsman.

The case of Arundhati Roy

When Arundhati Roy wrote an introduction to a book defending Mohammad Afzal Guru, the main accused in the December 13, 2001 attack on the Indian Parliament, she was more than un-equivocal in her anti-national views. By the way, what is the source of her revelations? Saba Naqvi Bhaumik, Bureau Chief of the Outlook magazine, had quoted names of certain foreign journals doing overtime to promote her image. (Hindustan Times, Chandigarh edition, 28/12/2006). The London based observer had raised the question, "Is Indian just jealous of Arundhati Roy" according to Saba, the Sunday Times carried a full-page article that equated Roy with Victoria Beckham both described as role models for young British women. What could be the vested interests of the Western Press in promoting the image of an Indian Woman? Are they not trying to manufacture consent about a woman who is neither a role model for Indians nor a representative of the deified Bhartiya Nari. Definitely, the interests of the globalized propaganda machinery are not those of Natural Selection but of Intelligent Design as visualized by Herman & Chomsky.

3 The Indianization Of Times Of India

Seth Ram Krishna Dalmia had purchased The Times of India from the British not for any patriotic reasons but as an enterprise to protect his other enterprises and as a weapon against those who could threaten his grand designs of an ever-expanding industrial empire. The extent to which he was aware of the use of the newspaper is crystal-clear in the following observations that he recorded in a slender volume:

"Today the newspapers are the biggest weapons, at least in no way less powerful than the atom bombs but God save us from many newspapers (Perhaps he was too conscious of the rivalry and the consequent threat to his empire), Blame, in a large measure, for the present day misery can be traced to the evil influence exerted by these. There is hardly any newspaper, which is not parochial and does not blindly support the party mandate irrespective of its merit or dismerit (sic). Even facts are twisted and the presenta-tion so coloured as to suit their purpose, and the masses accept the newspaper as propounding absolute truths, little imagining that they have emanated from common ordinary people, who have been sweating long hours just for their maintenance.[9] (This was his opinion about the journalists working for him or any other press baron)

The Early Struggle

R.K. Dalmia began his career as a broker in speculative commodities and was influenced to a great extent by Seth Baldeva Das Dudhavawalla who introduced him to the share market. At the time of his father's death, he was a lad of 22, already married and had the additional responsibility of the joint family. It was during the First World War that the young Dalmia was struggling hard to earn a livelihood. In his own words, "I was financially very hard hit; being a defaulter, I was despised and condemned as a criminal in the business world. I was not considered worthy of trust even for a paltry amount of five rupees by my relatives, who refused to advance me as a loan even this small sum."[10]

Nevertheless, he indulged in the speculative business of silver, earned some money, cleared his debts partially and again became penniless. In his own words, "After a few months I lost all my earnings and became penniless, yet I had credit in the market and managed to form a syndicate in partnership with my maternal uncle and some other influential businessmen during the First World War. We cornered all the silver (worth crores) available in the country and hoarded it in Calcutta and Bombay. We were in immediate need of over a crore of rupees in cash, but still were short of ten or fifteen lakhs. That amount could not be

---

[9] Some Notes & Reminiscences by R.K.Dalmia (P.60) published in 1948 by E.W.Dixon at The Times of India Press, Bombay.

[10] Ibid (P.10)

arranged even by mortgaging our silver and agreeing to pay 10 percent or 12 percent interest. We were on the horns of dilemma. Just at that moment I received a telephonic message from Sir Narcat Warren, Manager, Bank of Bengal (later amalgamated with the Imperial Bank of India) asking me to see him". The Manager wanted to know if Mr. Dalmia and his associates were willing to sell silver to the Government of India, for minting coins and if so, what quantity? This came as a boon to Mr. Dalmia who agreed to sell the commodity at a negotiated price. To quote him further, "I made several lakhs in that transation although my share was only 2 and 1/2 annas in the rupee. Likewise, we cornered silver many a time.[11]

Obviously, Mr. Dalmia had used a technique of financial management, which is still not taught at Harward. But what is more interesting to note is his strategy of repayment:

"During many periods of financial crisis in my life, I have not been in a position to pay my creditors their debts in full, debts that were time-barred and also not legally enforceable in a court of law due to speculative business. But when money came, I offered to repay the debts as far as it was possible for me to do so at the time. My creditors were overjoyed at this unexpected offer and gladly accepted part-payments, signing receipt in full and final clearance of all dues. There was no legal obligation and as I felt that I was absolved of moral obligations as well, there were no qualms of any kind. But some well meaning friends wonder why I do not care to liquidate the balance seeing that my charities given in one day on many occasions far exceeded in amount the total of my quarter of a century old debts. (enter Narcissus!) I do feel a punch, but I do not pay and I

---

[11] Ibid (P.24)

cannot say why I do not. Many of my old creditors and their sons also had died, still I paid to their heirs. Those of my old creditors who are living today do not remember the story and I also do not feel that I stand liable either in the court of man or God."[12]

Whatever be the reasons for his connivance, he never missed any opportunity to help the influential or those with a potential to emerge as leaders. When Motilal Nehru died, Dalmia wrote a letter to Jawaharlal Nehru enclosing a cheque of Rs.5000/-. In his own words, "I requested him to utilize that amount for his own sake and that if need be, I would send further amounts, or if he did not like to accept the money as a gift, he might treat is as a loan or in which-ever way he liked.[13]

In its issue dated 1 May 1992 *NAVABHARAT TIMES* (Bombay) had published certain extracts from R.K. Dalmia's auto-biography entitled, 'A short sketch of my life.' According to those extracts he had donated crores of rupees to the Indian National Congress before 1945 and it was Jamnalal Bajaj who had introduced both G.D. Birla and R.N. Goenka to Mahatma Gandhi. In the same extracts it was also quoted that he continued to give Rs.500/- p.m. to Subhas Chandra Bose for many years.

The Times of India Story

All the industrialists were surprised when Seth R.K Dalmia purchased *The Times of India* before independence. In his own words,

---

[12] Ibid (P.25)

[13] Ibid(P.52)

"such a British Paper was not available either to Indians or to Europeans. That was why the deal was struck secretly within so short a time. I further wanted to purchase The Statesman. For some reason or the other, I did not succeed in my attempt. When the deal for the purchase of the *Leader* was almost complete, Birlas appeared on the scene and purchased it. But Englishmen did not like to sell to Indians. In those days the biggest newspapers were *The Times of India* and *Statesman*. Despite strong opposition from Shanti Prasad and Jaidayal, I started the Delhi edition of *The Times of India, Dharmayug* and *Navabharat Times*. Thus all these papers are published simultaneously from Bombay and Delhi. The popularity and circulation of *The Times of India* would not have reached such a high peak but would have remained as leading newspapers in Maharashtra only, as is the case with *The Hindu* of Madras. I had a plan to make The Times of India a world renowned newspaper".[14]

He had deputed Sir Arthur Moore, ex-chief editor of the *Statesman* to London to purchase *The Times of India*. After prolonged stay in London, Sir Moore ultimately managed to send Sir Pearson, Managing Director of *The Times of India*. To quote Dalmia again, "when Sir Pearson asked," 'Do you want to buy for Rs.2 crores?' I put a blank cheque before him and asked him to fill it. Then he remarked, 'are you mad?' I replied, 'Look at the generosity of Indians'. The entire deal was finalized within 24 hours at little less that Rs.2 crores.' [15]

Sir Francis Low, the chief editor was drawing a monthly salary of Rs.10,000/- approx. When Dalmia purchased the

[14] The Times of India (Bombay) April 28, 1992

[15] The Times of India (Bombay) April 28, 1992

then "Old Lady of Boribunder". Frank Moraes who had distinguished himself as a war correspondence of The Times of India and was already an editor in Colombo succeeded Mr. Francis Low as the first Indian chief editor of *The Times of India*. However, Frank Moraes attributed this to sheer good luck. In his own words, "without being unduly modest, I would say that such success as I have attained as a journalist has been largely fortuitous. Luck, I believe, can sometimes play a decisive part in man's career. Had it not been for the war I would not have had the opportunity to enlarge my own experience and my own journalistic reputation such as it was at the time. Neither personally nor professionally have I ever played it safe, inclined as I am to accept equally the hazards of the short and the long chance. The war was a turning point in my career. Again, had independence not come a little before I was forty, I doubt if I would ever have been editor of The Times of India which until then was a sacrosanct preserve of the newspaper's senior British staff."[16]

Undoubtedly Frank Moraes was the most competent editor of his time, but the real reason of his selection by Dalmia would become more conspicuous only when we know the exact amount of salary offered to Mr. Moraes and the extent to which it was comparable with "that" drawn by the British editor. As time passed, Dalmia increasingly felt elevated as an intellectual with a convenient amnesia for his Marwari past. This was not possible without active association with intellectuals. He was not contented only as an employer of the English speaking editors but also wanted to associate with them in private parties. This prompted him to invite Frank Moraes for dinner. The situation has aptly

---

[16] 'Witness to an Era' by Frank Moraes (P.314)

been described by Dom Moraes in the Sunday Column of a Bombay based tabloid: "Having bought the Times and installed my father in position, he felt that they should have an amicable social relationship. He therefore, started asking my father to lunch and dinner at his house. These meals would and perhaps have been more friendly had it not been for the fact that while Dalmia ate his lunch off a silver thali he had my father, whom he considered untouchable served off earthenware, which was later broken so that nobody else could be contaminated by eating from it." To quote Dom Moraes further, "he also at some point wanted to start an airline. My father came to lunch when Dalmia was on a long distance call to a London agent. 'Dakotas?' he inquired. Yes, I want Dakotas. I will take half a dozen. No, a dozen'. Hanging up the receiver, he turned to my father and said, "Someone recommended that for my airline I should buy Dakotas so, as you heard, I have ordered a dozen. But Moraes, tell me, I do not know, what is a Dakotas? Father, who had flown in many, was amazed that Dalmia did not know."

"This was, I think" continues Dom, "the fist time the Marwari community became deeply interested in matters beyond textiles and so forth as money earners to the detriment of whatever attracted their interest, like the press. The Times passed from the hands of Dalmia into those of his relatives, the Jain family. My father resigned from it, but was then appointed by another Marwari, Ramnath Goenka, to edit a paper called the National Standard, which Goenka owned. It was renamed, the Indian Express and began to compete with the Times. How The Times of India changed hands is a different story altogether but perhaps it would be unfair not to quote Mr. Dalmia's account in this connection. According to him, "To arrange money, I was compelled to sell The Times of India and Jaipur Udyog". But there was no buyer in such circumstances. Then my son-in law, Shanti Prasad's Group of companies purchased the above concerns for Rs.2.1/2 crores. As the Reserve Bank was not accepting the payment, Shanti Prasad managed with Standard Chartered Bank to give guarantee to the Reserve Bank. The Reserve Bank thus had no alternative but to accept the payment. After the sell-out many parties came forward to purchase concerns at higher price. Since the transaction had already been concluded, it could not be reversed. I am glad that these companies are retained by Shanti Prasad's Group, as had they been sold to others, they would have gone forever.1 Little did he realize that they had already gone forever[17]. Ironically, the hoardings of the ad campaign for the matrimonial columns of the Times of India had summarized the copy after 45 long years. "Marriages are made in Heaven. Then we take-over."

Things have changed over the times. Mr. Ashok Jain succeeded his father Mr. Shanti Prasad Jain. He was in news due to alleged violations of FERA (Foreign Exchange Regulation Act) for which he was questioned by the Enforcement Directorate. The E.D. wanted him to testify on the charges against him after the Supreme Court rejected his plea for anticipatory bail. However, the E.D. constituted a Medical Board and allowed Mr. Ashok Jain to leave the country on the recommendations of the Board. Soon after the Apex Court rejected his plea for anticipatory bail, Mr. Ashok Jain launched on all-out offensive against the investigative agency in the print media through advertisements in which he claimed that he was 'continuously harassed, hounded and humiliated' by the E.D. His advertisements

---

[17] The Times of India (Bombay) April 28, 1992

described instances of 'abuse of power, harassment, violation of human rights, absence of checks and balances and lack of accountability' on the part of the E.D. Meanwhile, the TOI & the Economic Times devoted several columns every day on their front and inner pages condemning the E.D. for, among other things, "violating basic human rights". The TOI threw open its columns to the public to narrate accounts of perceived injustice done to them by State agencies like the E.D. It offered "the protection of public opinion" to those who wanted to talk freely and frankly about such experiences.

Although the FERA probe against Jain was highlighted in the two newspapers published by Mr. Jain's Company, there was hardly any news report or editorial comment on the subject in other national dailies. The Delhi Union of Journalists (DUJ) issued a statement condemning, "the use of journalists and newspapers to whip up frenzy on caste and regional lines on behalf of their managements facing charges of financial skullduggery." On June 30, 1998 the DUJ said that journalists' dignity and authority were being eroded as a consequence of their being reduced to public relations officers of management in their personal wars. Referring to the TOI, the DUJ noted that journalists were being virtually railroaded into writing motivated stories. The DUJ appealed to the Press Council of India to look into the orchestrated campaign by the management of *The Times of India* in this matter.

Unfortunately the E.D. was not allowed to explain its position to the press as a gag order passed by the Delhi High Court, in a case filed by Ashok Jain restrained the E.D. from doing so. Commenting on the gag order, Mr. Ajit Bhattacharjea, Director of the Press Institute of India observed, "It is most unfortunate that the E.D. is unable to speak up for itself to clear its reputation. This fact is unknown to the general public, which thinks that the E.D. has no answer to the charges. This predicament of the E.D. should be highlighted."[18] The adverse media reports on the E.D. flooded the headlines soon after it raided the TOI offices in Mumbai, Calcutta and New Delhi in the third week of January (1998). The E.D. also searched and seized documents from Jain's cabin in Bombay Hospital where he was admitted soon after the Supreme Court denied him anticipatory bail against possible arrest by the E.D.

In another development, Shashi Hoon, a Toronto-based businessman who, in a statement to the E.D. during 1997 confirmed that he had accompanied Alok Kumar Jain, brother of Ashok Jain (of Bennett Coleman & Co.), and Congress President, Sitaram Kesri in 1967 to open an account is Barclays Bank London, in the name of Kesri, was reported to have been found dead, 'under mysterious circumstances' in Toronto. According to newspaper reports, Hoon was required to give a statement before E.D. officials on January 25, but was found dead on January 22, a day before he was due to board the plane to India. Officially, E.D. sources maintained that no date was fixed for Hoon's meeting with the officials and that Hoon was to visit India on a private mission.

According to June 20 - July 03, 1998 issue of *Frontline*, after the summary dismissal of H.K.Dua, the then Editorial Adsviser of the TOI allegedly for failure to help Ashok Jain in the FERA investigation, the Times Management persuaded top level journalists in the newspaper to sign an affidavit/letter expressing their dissatisfaction with Mr. Dua's editorial competence and integrity. Although one or two

---

18 FRONTLINE, Feb.21 - March 06, 1998 Issue.

people may have signed it, others refused to do so. When contacted by *Frontline*, Mr. Dileep Padgaonkar (who had rejoined the Times group with a corporate designation) replied that he was not aware of any such move. "It is absolutely rubbish as far as I am concerned" he added. Contrary to Mr. Padgaonkar's unequivocal reply, certain other persons talked of pressure tactics.

The Editors Guild issued the following statement on May 29, 1998 signed by its president, Mr. Vinod Mehta, "The removal of the Editor of a premier newspaper by an abrupt and premature termination of his contract without any explanation has grave implications for the freedom of the press which is central to the ethos of any democratic society and thus becomes a public issue". It added, "The Guild has in the past few years been dismayed by trends suggestive of managerial interference into day-to-day editorial functions. Mr. Dua's exit again brings into sharp focus the deteriorating relationship between editors and proprietors. These anxieties are heightened by reports that Mr. Dua was removed not for professional reasons, but because of his unwillingness to support the owner's collateral interest that had little to do with the conduct of the newspapers".

In a joint statement issues by exemplary MPs like Geeta Mukherjee, Gurudas Dasgupta, V.K.Alagh and prominent journalists like B.G.Verghese, Kuldip Nayar, M.V.Kamat, Prabhash Joshi, N.K.Trikha, N.Bhaskar Rao and Hiranyamay Karlekar, it was observed, "The entire range of developments raises serious questions about the role of journalists and the use of newspapers by those who run and manage them. All those interested in the freedom of the press and newspaper standards must take cognizance of this deplorable development and ensure that the vital role that newspaper and journalists play in a democracy is not per-verted."19

After Mr. Ashok Jain's demise, his widow Mrs.Indu Jain took-over. Forbes magazine had included her name in the list of 27 Indian billionaires. Being a conventional Indian widow, she is more inclined towards religion and salvation rather than corporate management, which is governed by her two sons viz; Sameer and Vineet. The former received international media attention when Mr. Nicholas Coleridge published his celebrated work, 'The Paper Tigers' that high-lighted Mr. Sameer Jain's style of functioning. For the second time, he was in news when he introduced the concept of paid news for which the coinage 'page three' emerged as a popular euphemism. Once again, Mr. Sameer Jain was in news when he diluted the credentials of the Time of India from an editorial product into a consumer product like soap, toothpaste or a brand name for a hair-removing-cream. As if this were not enough, he created history for the fourth time when he deconstructed the conventional chair of the chief editor into a bevy of columnists. Besides, the Times Group has drawn some amount of flak for a scheme called 'Media-Net' which other firms can use to purchase editorial coverage in the daily. Of late, the Times Group has started a focused practice on acquiring clients under a programme named 'Private Treaties' in which PR and advertisements are provided in return for purchase of client's company shares. The latest in the list of controversies is the case of Pradyuman Maheshwari, who used to criticize the TOI on his 'Mediaah Weblog'. He received a legal threat from the TOI after a posting that highlighted the newspaper's deal with Reuters related to TV. Even though

------

19 FRONTLINE, June 20 July 03, 1998 Issue

another newspaper picked up the same story, Maheshwari was unwilling to fight. He withdrew the posting and apologized. On March 7, 2004 he received a legal notice asking him to remove 19 blogposts related to the Times, or the company would take legal action. According to Maheshwari much of what upset the Times was his criticism of its Media-Net initiative where businessman can actually buy photos and profile stories in the Times' editorial section, what it calls *edvertorials.*

While Maheshwari was reluctant to fight in the Court, the Indian blogosphere was prompt enough to rise to the occasion. One anonymous blogger spared no time to setup '*Mediaha*' a blog that contains the 19 blogposts in question (which were withdrawn by Maheshwari) as well as the seven-page legal notice from the Times.

Quoting Sevanti Ninan in this connection, the Online Journalism Review has recorded. "The print media here has a very thin skin. Newspaper proprietors are wary of letting staff write about other newspapers in case the scrutiny is turned on them too." Commenting on the episode, Shashidhar Nanjundiah has observed ".....India claims to be as much a democracy as the United States is, but let's face one of the many differences. In the State someone would have slapped a PIL on the Times by now for its unethical practices and misleading the public. It's time we woke up." - OJR.

As an accumulated result of these controversies and myopic initiatives, intellectual editors were devalued as eccentrics fit only to work as copywriters under brand managers who occasionally directed them to highlight the civil rights of gays and lesbians as also the human rights of ex-humans like the terrorists. Being the largest circulated English daily, its cost of production is heavily subsidized by the advertisements and paid news. Hence, Mr. Sameer Jain is in a privileged position to dictate the price game that has also constrained the other market players to keep their price tag at the minimum. When the Bhaskar Group initiated its pre-launch ad campaign for DNA, Mr. Sameer Jain launched, *Mumbai Mirror* shortly before the inaugural issue of the D.N.A. with a Public announcement, 'your search for a complete newspaper stops here'. This gave an impression that the on going campaign launched by the *DNA* was meant for *Mumbai Mirror* and not the *DNA*. The owners of DNA being themselves Marwaris, spared no time to sue The TOI in the Court of Law. Thus, Mr. Sameer Jain was in the limelight for the 5th time. Of late, they (the TOI Group) have launched a TV News Channel called *Times Now* and *Entertainment Network, India Ltd* that runs *Radio Mirchi*. The group's net worth is \$2.4 billion, the main business is media owned by Bennett Coleman and Co. Ltd but the following corporate entities who own more than 1% of the paid-up capital, do not appear to be media players:

   I. Sanmati Properties Ltd., Times House, 4th Floor, 7 BSZ Marg, New Delhi-110 002;

   II. Bharat Nidhi Ltd. Times House, 4th Floor, 7 BSZ Marg, New Delhi-110 002;

   III. P.N.B. Finance and Industries Ltd. 10, Daryaganj, New Delhi-110 002;

   IV. Camac Commercial Company Ltd., 8 Camac Street, Kolkata-700 017;

   V. Arth Udyog Ltd., Times House, 4th Floor, 7 BSZ Marg, New Delhi-110 002;

   VI. Punjab Properties Ltd., 10, Daryaganj, New Delhi-110 002;

   VII. T.M. Investment, 8 Camac Street, 14th Floor, Kolkata-700 017.

VIII.Ashok Viniyog Ltd., 8 Camac Street, 14th Floor, Kolkata-700 017.

Now the million-clichéd question is what separates the Indian Press from the corporate lobby as also what integrates it with the same? Mr. Sameer Jain! Are you listening?

4 Indian Express: The Myth And Reality

When Frank Moraes was appointed as the Chief Editor of the Times of India in 1950, little did he realize that his employer would be serving a prison term and the embarrassment of serving a convict would be so much stigmatizing as to make him quit the job only to be hooked by another Marwari. This other Marwari was Ramnath Goenka whose enthusiasm to compete with *The Times of India* had already become a legend during his peak of glory. However the name of his paper was *National Standard* which was subsequently renamed, *The Indian Express*. While the relationship between Goenka and Frank Moraes was quite all right, Dom Moraes has a different story about his own experience.

"In 1962 he (Goenka) came to London where I lived, telephoned me, and said that he thought the standard of English in Indian journalism was appalling, except for my father's. He wished, therefore, to employ a number of young English journalists to go and help my father in India. I thought it a demented idea, and asked if my father has been consulted about it. 'I never do anything without consulting your father' he replied. So I in turn consulted that great English journalist, James Cameron. James was an old friend of my father's as now of mine and his first reaction was, 'All your father's staff will resign when they hear about this. Has your man Goenka asked him?' I replied that he said he had.

James and I collected six young English journalists and Goenka invited them all to lunch. Then he offered them high salaries, cars, flats and servants. Mostly stunned by their luck, they accepted. One Stephen Hugh - Jones of the *Guardian* signed up on the spot. He left for India almost immediately. In the meantime Goenka said to me, "All the young men are good, but the old man, Cameron is very good. Make him an offer". I said, "don't you realize who he is? He will never come".

Huge - Jones then arrived in Bombay. This was the first time my father had heard of Goenka's activities in London, and he phoned me in total shock. "Is Goenka out of his mind?" he asked, a question I felt he should have been better equipped to answer than me. For as James had predicted, his whole editorial staff had threatened to resign if any Englishmen were hired. Eventually a compromise was reached. Stephen Hugh - Jones being already in situ, would remain, but the rest were to be told that their contracts were cancelled."

In 1980 when Dom Moraes decided to stay in India, he wanted to publish a colour magazine for the international market. So he approached Goenka with the proposal as he had all the colour machinery required for the purpose. Goenka welcomed him effusively to the *Express* and offered him to edit the Sunday supplement of the *Express* as the colour machines were out of order. Recalling the experience Dom writes, "I didn't know this was because I had recently finished a biography of Indira Gandhi and he assumed wrongly, that I was close to her and could obtain favours for him from her. While the colour machines were being set right I edited the Sunday supplement of The Express. But not for long. Goenka discovered that I was not a favourite of Gandhi's. I ceased to be one of his blue-eyed boys, and I resigned. I also discovered that he was a disciple of Maharishi Mahesh Yogi's, that the colour equipment was a gift from the Maharishi, that the mechanics who came from overseas to repair it were all from the Maharishi's ashram in Switzerland, and that Goenka believed that he could levitate".

What Dom learnt from Goenka

Dom Moraes failed to understand how his father managed to work with Goenka for over two decades. In his own words "But from 1947 onward my father worked with Marwaris, and perhaps he had come to understand how they functioned. I certainly couldn't. But the experience with Goenka was valuable in so far as it convinced me that the best way for a journalist to operate in this country was as a freelance.

The background of R.N. Goenka

Very few people are aware that Mr. Ramnath Goenka (RNG) who had adopted his grandson (daughter's son) as his heir was himself an adoptee. When the infant Goenka was six months, he lost his mother and was adopted by the widow of Seth basantlal Goenka. After graduation from BHU, he joined the business of his maternal uncles at Calcutta. It is perhaps a coincidence that his maternal uncles - Babu Prahlad Rai and Babu Sagarmal were also Dalmias. At the age of 18 his uncles recommended him to a Madras based firm (cotton textile) where he was accepted as an agent. After three years he launched a partnership firm at Hyderabad in 1925. In 1926, the Governor of Madras nominated him as a member of the Madras legislative Council. This was the beginning of his political career. In 1927 he became Secretary of the Independent Party. It was during this time that he opposed the Simon Commission tooth and nail and emerged as a hero. Subsequently, he joined the Bombay Company Ltd. as its Chief Salesman where he continued till 1936. He left Bombay in 1936 to join as a partner of a Madras based firm that dealt with the Stock Exchange.

His political graph

In the year 1946 he was elected to the Constituent Assembly. In the same year he visited Eurupe, America and Canada as a member of the Delegation of the Indian and Eastern Newspaper Society. In the year 1951 he was elected as President of IENS. He was Chairman of PTI during 1952-53 and became its director in 1963, the position which he held throughout his life. Besides, he was Chairman of the Punjab National Bank during 1952-53. In 1971 he was elected as an M.P. with the supoort of the then JANASANGH (the prototype of BJP) from Vidisha. He was a member of the All India Congress Committee in 1969 before the vertical split of the party at the instance of Mrs.Indira Gandhi.

Goenka's Pulpdom

The Indian Express was founded at Madras in the year 1931 by Dr.P. Varadrajulu Naidu who sold it to Sadanand after one year. Sadanand also owned the FPJ in Bombay and found it difficult to manage both the papers. He approached C.Rajgopalachari in April 1932 with a request to take over the Indian Express. However, Rajaji suggested him to contact K.Santhanam who had just been released from prison as a Satyagrahi. On Rajaji's advice Santhanam accepted the editorship of the Indian Express. Thus the Indian Express became a morning paper and an organ for the Congress Party. Shortly, a sister Tamil daily - the Dinamani was added which outstripped all its rivals in Tamil journalism. However, the Indian Express fell into a financial crisis and it finally passed into the hands of Ramnath Goenka.[20] In 1934 Goenka had purchased debentures of The Free Press of India Ltd. (Madras). This was the company that owned the Indian Express that time. Eventually, he purchased all the 2.5 lakhs of shares of his company.

The million dollar question that confronts us here is the financial source that enables the Chief Salesman of the Bombay Company Ltd. to first purchase the debentures and then to purchase 2.5 lakhs of its shares. It was in 1934 that he had purchased debentures and had left The Bombay Company Ltd. in 1936 to join a Madras based firm that dealt with the stock exchange. It appears that the shares were purchased either late or in gradual succession and the source of finance could be either market borrowings or the occasional 'windfalls' of speculative earnings at the stock exchange. Whatever be the reality, RNG continued to excel in financial management through the exclusive Marwari technique of 'transferred caps'. However, the real breakthrough came in 1952-53 when he became Chairman of The Punjab National Bank. This was followed by a pre-budget leak or hunch regarding steel scrips during late 50's that transformed the empire of 'transferred caps' into the three-

---

[20] Journalism in India by Rangaswamy Parthsarthy (p.253)

dimensional reality of liquid cash. Politically, he remained dormant during Nehru's regime but assumed significance as a member of the ICC, when the Congress Party was split vertically. Contrary to the prevailing myth, it was during Lal Bahadur Shastri's regime (and not of Mrs.Gandhi's) that Govt. action was first initiated against the pulpdom of RNG. Since then, a game of 'musical chairs' continued between RNG and umpteen enforcement agencies of the Govt. of India till he breathed his last on 5th of October 1991.

Way back in 1973, the Bhabtosh Datta Committee on newspaper economics went into the fiannces of major newspapers in the country. Relevant extracts regarding RNG's empire from the said Committee's report have been reproduced below:

I. Till 1973, the Indian Express group alone accounted for more that 25 per cent of the total amount outstanding to banks from newspapers.

II. Apart from this, the newspapers have been collecting deposits from the public without giving them any say in the newspaper companies. "A disturbing trend revealed in our analysis is that some of these newspaper undertakings have been resorting to this form of raising non-banking deposits from the public. No detailed accounts of the deposits are kept by the companies, raising doubts about their source. To the extent data could be collected by the committee, an annexure was made regarding the fixed deposits obtained by the newspaper organizations which were outstanding. It may be observed therefrom that the Indian Express group tops the list (on April 30, 1971), owing to the public Rs.1,067 lakh on such account. The Indian Express was during all this period showing losses and it remains to be examined how the public came to invest their saving in a losing

company in preference to profitable forms of investment".

III. In the case of some newspaper undertakings, the
amounts expended on land and building were consider-
ably in excess of the requirements of a newspaper business and were, therefore, in the nature of investment in
immovable properties unrelated to newspaper business.
This was obvious from the fact that the gross rental income of 63 undertakings from such properties were 143
lakh during 1973 of which 114 lakh related only to the
Indian Express group. The tabulation revealed that the
Indian Express group and Hindustan Times Ltd. acquired large properties during just six years, though
these were not required for newspaper business.

IV. The current assets in the case of the Indian Express
group contained a significant amount of inter- company
transactions under the head of loans and advances. On
the current liabilities side also, there were inter-company transactions more or less of the same magnitude.
Thus, both the sides of the balance sheet have been inflated to this extent. It appears that large funds have
been diverted by the Indian Express to be used for purposes unrelated to newspaper business. Till 1973, such
diversion of funs amounted to Rs.11 crore in the case of
The Indian Express group.

V. The presence of so many different types of companies, partnerships, trusts etc. and the complexity of the
interlocking makes it difficult for any one to obtain a
clear view of the finances of the Indian Express group.
Therefore, the committee suggests that a proper probe
is made into the nature of interlocking, its purpose, its
outcome. *Such an enquiry has to be done on the basis of*

The first series of the CBI raids on the business and residential premises of the Express group took place in February 1965. Later, the company Law Board inspected the books of accounts of four Express group companies during 1969. These included - Indian Express Newspapers (Bombay) Private Ltd., Andhra Prabha Private Ltd., Indian Express (Madurai) Private Ltd. and Express Newspapers Private Ltd. The Inspection revealed false and fabricated entries of purchases of newsprint by the group companies from a company called Messers Radha Company, 7 Lyons Range Calcutta, which on investigation, was found to be non-existent. The inspection also revealed fabrication of accounts with a view to raising loans and advances from the Punjab National Bank and The Indian Bank Ltd. The fictitious operations were aimed at augmenting Andhra Prabha's working capital. Not only was the loan secured by misrepresenting the newsprint stock, but the loan thus secured was never actually utilized for the purpose intimated to the bank. It was actually diverted to Express Newspaper Private Ltd. which advanced it further to other subsidiaries, which in turn, used the funds for speculation in the share market.

The inspectors of Company Law Board had recorded their observations as follows:

"Had the banks known the correct position relating to newsprint stocks, they would certainly not have extended the overdraft facility". The inspectors recommended investigations under section 237B of the Companies Act and on the basis of Company Law Board's advice the CBI registered a case for investigation under Sections 120 B, 420, read with 477 A and 420 of Indian Penal Code on.19th of April

1971 as crime No.2 of 1971. This was the second historic instance of criminal significance in the brothel of pulpdom of free India, the first being the infamous Times of India episode that resulted in jail term for R.K. Dalmia.

After registration of the case, the Chief Presidency Magistrate, Madras issued a warrant under section 96 of the Code of Criminal Procedure on June 7, 1971 for search of the premises of these companies and of the residences of the managing director/directors. RNG moved the Madras High court for quashing the Chief Presidency Magistrate's order. However, the petition was dismissed first by a single judge of the High court on 22 September, 1971 and then by the Division Bench of the High Court on 20th of March 1973. The High Court did not grant any stay of the proceedings or injunction against the arrest and prosecution of RNG. He went in appeal against the Madras High Court Order to the Supreme Court in 1973 where it remained pending for 13 long years. However, the Supreme Court dismissed it on 21st of November 1986. It was observed by their Lordships, "we do not think that it would be proper to interfere in the order passed by the High court." This order was issued jointly by Mr. Justice M.B. Thakkar and Mr. Justice B.C. Ray on November 21, 1986. However, RNG was never arrested despite no injunction against his arrest by the High court and no intervention of the Supreme Court against the High Court's observation. All said and done, RNG breathed his last on 5th of October 1991 as an "honorable man" and an exalted press baron.

The Criminal graph of Goenka's Ambitions

Perhaps no other press baron has caused so much headache to the Company Law Board than the Late RNG and his controversial successors who continued to invoke the Board's intervention even in such matters as the maintenance of internal democracy in the corporate entity. The first major inspection of the Express group of companies by the Board was conducted in 1969. The Company Law Board ordered yet another major inspection of the Indian Express Newspapers (Bombay) Private Ltd. vide letter No.21/46/81-CI.II of December 3, 1981. This inspection revealed the following atrocities:

I.   Contravention of Section 209, 292, 297, 383 A, 314(IB), 209(I), 209 (II) etc. of Companies Act.

II. The need for a thorough investigation into violations of not only the Income Tax Act and Wealth Tax Act, but also that of Foreign Exchange Regulation Act.

The findings of this inspection were as follows:

I.   "ACE Pvt. Ltd." one of the group companies, was suddenly delinked from the chain. This enabled RNG to acquire controlling interest in this former subsidiary which owns all the real estate assets of the chain at Bombay, Madras, Bangalore and Delhi. The entire share capital of ACE was transferred personally to Ram nath Goenka. Thus the real estate valued at crores of Rupees was transferred from the Newspaper Publishing Company into the personal name of Ram Nath Goenka.

II. It was found that Ram Nath Goenka had been transferring huge funds from the Indian Express Newspaper (Bombay) Pvt. Ltd. to various sister companies which in turn, had been utilizing these funds for speculative activities in the stock market.

III. It was found that massive amounts of money from the Indian Express (Bombay) Private Ltd. had been transferred to RNG's personal account and he had been using the funds for speculation in the stock market. According to inspectors he had been pocketing the profits earned and paid no interest to the Company from which the funds were siphoned-out.

IV. The inspectors found that the newsprint consumption account had been manipulated so as to conceal a fair view of the state of affairs of the Company which claimed 15% of the total newspaper circulation in the country.

V. The inspectors found that the company was defrauding the govt. by not paying income-tax and wealth-tax dues, though it was falsely recording the liability as having been discharged in its account books. The inspectors recommended that the matter be referred to the Income Tax Department for appropriate action.

VI. It was found that the company did not pay the requisite customs duty on newsprint. An amount of Rs. 143.34 lakh was due from the company against customs duty as recorded by inspectors.

VII.It was found that the Indian Express (Bombay) Private Ltd. had opened a foreign account in which it deposited the sale proceeds of newspapers, periodicals as well as the advertisement revenue earned from foreign sources. According to the inspectors, the company, in operating this account failed to comply with the various provisions of FERA. The inspectors recommended that the matter be referred to the Reserve Bank of India for appropriate action.

VIII.Yet another fraud discovered by this Inspection Team related to the transfer of a sum of Rs.4,80,000/- to a certain company for purchase of land on behalf of Ram Nath Goenka. However, during inspection, the inspectors could not find any particulars of this land "leaving an unmistakable impression that the transaction could have been fictitious."

IX. Another item suggesting possible fraud related to the transfer of Rs.2,96,355/- from the Indian Express (Bombay) Private Ltd. to a certain trust called "Dharan Pratisthan Vedic Science". In this case also, the inspectors could not locate the whereabouts of the trust.

The Second Major Inspection

The second major inspection of RNG's pulp Dom by the Company Law Board was undertaken in 1985. The Deputy Director of the Company Law Board had inspected Messers Indian Express Newspapers (Bombay) Private Ltd. from October 10, 1985 to November 27, 1985. According to the dossier dated March 7, 1986 prepared by the deputy Director of the Company Law Board, "Having regards to the assets, the turnover and the power which the companies owned by Ram Nath Goenka wield on the news media and public opinion, there is substantial public interest involved in the affairs of this group and also the group of companies is of such a nature as to involve substantial public interest in terms of the Income Tax Act."

Following is the illustrative (not exhaustive) list of violations highlighted in the aforesaid inspection report:

I. The Goenka company has neither paid its wealth-tax liability nor even ascertained the said liability as it claims to have been advised by its own legal experts that the said levy is unconstitutional. But the company has not challenged the wealth tax levy in any court so far. The implication of this finding is that the citizens of India can refuse to pay tax by simply taking the stand that the tax is unconstitutional, without bothering to test their claim in a court.

II. The Goenka group had debited to newsprint consumption account the variation in the price of newsprint on loan from its subsidiaries. Customs duty running into crores of Rupees remains unpaid to the Government. The inspection report says that the company may not be in a position to pay the customs duty withheld by it "if it is ordered to pay it". The implication of this finding being the fact that the Government had lost crores of Rupees just to promote Goenka's own brand of "freedom of the press".

III. The Goenka group operated a sterling account with the London branch of State Bank of India but did not submit the prescribed return to the Reserve Bank of India as required by the RBI's approval letter. The implication being the possibility of a serious violation of Foreign Exchange Regulation Act.

IV. The report of the group company's directors falsely stated and misrepresented the ownership of the shares of the company and therefore "appears to have invited serious violations of various laws".

V. The Express Newspapers Private Ltd. has been making loans to subsidiaries to enable them to purchase shares in the stock market and the transfer of funds has been prolonged on an on-going basis from one to the other company in order to depress the profitability of the group and to confer advantage on individuals at the expense of the newspaper companies. In other words, money has been siphoned-off by RNG for his personal benefit and the benefit of the close relatives.

VI. As stated in the earlier report, the assets of the newspaper company in the form of real estate have been suddenly transferred to a subsidiary, viz., ACE Private Ltd. which, in turn, was delinked from the group. As a result, substantial real estates owned by Express Newspapers Private Ltd. at Bombay, Madras, Bangalore and Delhi were transferred to ACE and in turn, were taken over by Ram Nath Goenka and his relatives.

According to the report "How the delinking of the subsidiaries is in the interest of the company is not clear. The company is a legal entity distinct from its shareholders, but in the process of regrouping it has lost control over valuable real estate and the benefit of the escalation in its price or income there from which would now go to RNG and his relatives. Thus, while rearranging the group for the benefit of a few individuals the newspaper company has lost crores of Rupees".

After Indira Gandhi returned to power in January 1980, RNG was scared of a possible vendetta, so he pretended to be, 'reformed' and beamed quite a good number of "friendly" signals which she ignored. However, an inspection of Indian Express Newspapers (Bombay) Private Ltd. was ordered on February 3, 1981. Relevant extracts of the said inspection report are as follows [21]:

I. Indian Express Newspapers (Bombay) Private Ltd. is engaged in printing and publication of newspapers and periodicals in English and other Indian languages some of which have very wide circulation and considerable influence over news media and public opinion. It is a closely held but large-sized private limited company with a paid-up capital of Rs.86.5 lakh, assets of Rs.16 crore (book value) and turnover of Rs,31.74 crore. It is

---

[21] News Today, Madas, 18 December 1986, Editor, T.R.Rao.

registered under the MRTP Act (before the ceiling of the MRTP companies was raiseds from Rs.25 crore to Rs.100 crore). It has five branches situated at Ahmedabad, Delhi, Chandigarh, Madras and Calcutta. (In the last named centre, there is no publication but the branch office is used to effect inter-company money transfers). It has three wholly owned subsidiaries namely, The Indian Express (Madurai) Private Ltd. (IEM), Traders Private Ltd. (Bombay) (TPL) and Andhra Prabha Private Ltd. (APPL).

II. The total assets and turnover of the holding company together with   the subsidiaries are much higher. It is quite an empire by itself which is controlled by a single individual, Shri Ram Nath Goenka. Having regards to the assets, the turnover and the power which the company wields over news media and the public opinion, it may be stated that though a private limited company, there is substantial public interest involved in the affairs of the company.

III. Ram Nath Goenka is closely associated with the company. He is the moving spirit behind the company. He is Chairman and Managing Director of the company, but his shareholding in the company is an insignificant part of the total subscribed and paid-up capital of Rs.86.5 lakh which consist of equity capital of Rs.60 lakh and preference capital of Rs.26.5 lakh, Goenka is holding only seven (7) preference share of the face value of Rs. 6000/-. He is not holding a single equity share. The whole of the share capital, both equity and preference, is held by his relatives, firms, private limited companies and trusts which are all controlled by him and in which he is interested. (In other words, Goenka really and effectively owns the Indian Express Group, yet for the purpose of the law he is not the owner! His firms, trusts and companies are the owners for the purpose of taxation).

IV. But for the income earned by the company from the Express Tower building at Nariman Point, the company has not been a viable unit. It has been making losses in its publication business and only in the year 1984-85 it made a profit because of the strike in the Times of India which led to increased circulation for it.

V. The rental income received by the company in three years were: 1982-83 - Rs.161.50 lakh, 1983-84 - Rs.229.19 lakh and 1984-85 - Rs.264.87 lakh.

VI. In addition, the company received interest-free deposits from its tenants. In 1982-83, such deposits came to Rs.60.68 lakh, in 1983-84 to Rs.193.43 lakh and in 1984-85 Rs.195.61 lakh. These interest-free deposits have given a substantial fillip to the cash flow of the company.

VII.Though a closely-held private limited company, the shareholders have not received any dividend. (They have received other benefits). It has not paid dividend on its preference shares capital as required by law except in the year 1960-61. The arrears of dividends on preference shares for the year ended 30-04-1962 to 31-01-1985 are 54.64 lakh.

Notional Debits

The inspection report also highlighted Goenka's innovative technique of notional debits for the purpose of cheating both the government and the employees. According to the inspection report, the Goenka company has been debiting huge amounts in newsprint consumption account every year, describing them as variation in the price of newsprint on loan from subsidiaries and the ruling prices. *It was also found to be debiting the customs duty while it did not pay the sums which were described as having been paid.* As a result, newsprint consumption account was inflated and the profits were depressed. "The net result is that the annual account of the company does not show the true and fair view of the state of affairs of the Goenka company at the close of each year" says the finding. After detailing the notional debit entries made in the imported newsprint consumption account from 1980-81 to 1984-85, the inspection report goes on to identify the action required:

"The corresponding credit (on debit entries) was neither passed on   to the companies concerned nor accounted for in the value of the newsprint as an income in the profit and loss account. Considering the tax rate of 67%, the company has gained by way of tax not paid to the extent of over Rs.60 lakh in five years. This may be referred to the Income Tax authorities for their information and action as deemed necessary".

Customs duty on newsprint was introduced in March 1981. RNG challenged it under Article 32 of the Constitution in the Supreme Court alleging that the levy infringed his fundamental rights under Article 19 of the Constitution.

When the petition came up before the Supreme Court, he was asked to give security for the duty payable in the event of the case going against him. Goenka, in turn, asked the public sector bank to release the property so that it could be given as security to the Union of India. The State Bank of India refused to oblige because "the accounts of the company and its subsidiaries are irregular". The Marwari Press Baron cleverly resorted to a via media and gave an undertaking to the Court that he would not alienate or encumber his properties, pending disposal of case.

Subsequently, he strategically bifurcated his companies into *newspaper companies* and *non-newspaper companies*, transferred the assets of the former to the latter and ultimately delinked the same from the newspaper business for his own benefit and that of his relatives. In this connection, the inspection report has recorded, "it will be seen that a sum of Rs.143.34 lakh is payable by the company and the aggregate amount payable along with its two subsidiaries is Rs.339.85 lakh."

Despite inherent contradictions in Goenka's brand of freedom of the press, he emerged as a towering crusader due mainly to his anti- establishment approach. This approach, as we have seen, was not rooted in any missionary zeal but was a continuum of a press baron's anger who either failed to extract favours for his empire from the Government or could not dictate his terms to the then Prime Minister with a view to wielding his own clout as also to satisfy his megalomania.

Goenka was never considered a very good pay-master to his editorial staff. The only exceptions were the luminous Chief-editors whom he had engaged for a particular cause and period, to say nothing about the cute girls who surrounded the press baron. Prabhash Joshi, the founder editor of JANASATTA (The Hindi counterpart of Indian Express) and the second highest paid Hindi journalist of the country during 1980's (the first being the late Rajendra Mathur) paid tributes to RNG thus:

"इस देश में प्रेस को फनफनाती हुई आज़ादी है और इसकी ताकत से शासकों के सिंहासन डोलते हैं तो इसका श्रेय किसी साहू, जैन, बिरला या आयंगार को नहीं है । किसी एक व्यक्ति को अगर यह श्रेय दिया जा सकता है तो रामनाथ गोयनका को

जनसत्ता ६ अक्टूबर १९९१"

["In this country the press is vibrantly free and it is powerful enough to dwindle the chairs of rulers. The credit for this does not go any SAHU JAIN, BIRLA or AAYANGAR. If this can be credited to any person, it is R.N.Goenka alone].
Jansatta, 06th October 1991

Perhaps Prabhashji was not aware of the following:

I. On September 1, 1970 certain Member of parliament sought information on the CBI enquiry into the malpractices indulged in by the maze of interlocked firms held by RNG. The written reply to the question was in two parts. The first part contained the text of the CBI chargesheet filed in 1965 when Indira Gandhi was not the Prime Minister. According to the reply the case was pending before a Calcutta court against six of Goenka's jute purchasing officers. The main charge against them was that they entered into a criminal conspiracy to defraud the National Company by recording fictitious purchases. The second part of the reply contained the text of the FIR filed by an Under Secretary in the Government of India directing CBI to investigate the huge diversion of funds from the National Company, owned by a variety of Goenka's newspaper companies, for purchasing shares of the Indian Iron & Steel Company.

The National Company, with a nominal capital of a few lakhs of Rupees managed to obtain a loan of about Rs.5 crore from the State Bank of India and other public financial institutions "to dabble in stock market speculation and purchases". Mr. K.V.Raghunath Reddy, the Minister concerned clarified to the Parliament that an additional amount of Rs.3 crore, used by RNG for his 'adventure' comprised "fictious money". The modus operandi for this was through issuing what are called the public

delivery orders against non-existing jute goods. The entire amount of Rs.8 crore was deployed for grabbing Indian Iron & Steel Company shares.

For reasons known only to God & RNG he failed to
take over TISCO. But the truth remains that what was
stated in the Parliament by a Minister of the Union of
India long before the advent of the Emergency has not
been found false or malicious by any court in its final
verdict.

The Central Government appointed Mr. Rajgopal, a
top ranking officer in the Finance Ministry, to follow up
the Minister's assurance to Parliament that there would
be no attempt to whitewash the happenings in RNG's
empire. The offier submitted his report in October, 1972.
According to this report RNG had raised a total amount
of Rs.23 crore during 1966-71 for his many non-newspaper adventures. There were straight borrowings from
the State Financial Institutions including banks and
about Rs.11 crore from the public by way of deposits
which were not secured either against the shares of the
company or its debentures. At the end of 1970, RNG
formed a partnership firm called Express Traders. The
investigator thought that all the assets of the newspaper
empire, including the real estate properties had been
transferred to Express Traders. At a later stage, RNG re-
futed this charge but he did not inform the public as to
who owned what in his intricate and interlocked empire
of companies, firms and private trusts. Subsequently,
the Bhabtosh Dutt Committee on Newspaper Economics
reported in 1975 that it found the job of understanding
the Goenka empire so exasperating that it could only
recommend "a separate and thorough investigation into
the affairs of this express group, bringing together the

data available with different authorities and examine further the way in which the newspaper profits have been used or misused."

II. During the election battle between Krishna Menon & Kriplani in 1962 the Express chain launched a campaign of character assassination against Menon. Nehru, who campaigned for Menon had censured the attitude of the Press baron. According to D.R.Mankekar, "Here was a classic example of how a newspaper campaign, over-done, boomeranged. A substantial segment of the voters in this constituency consisted of an affluent intelligentsia, generally conservative in their politics, but sensitive in their perceptions, who left to themselves, would have voted against what they described as a "fellow traveler." The unduly aggressive and unseemly attacks unleashed at Krishna Menon by the Express, however roused their wrath and sympathy in favour of the "crypto-communist", as the Goenka-Moraes edits and news items labeled Krishna Menon and drove them in hordes to the polling booths to vote for Krishna Menon.

When the results of the bye-election were declared and it was found that the Express candidate had been defeated, Goenka was truly crest-fallen and penitent, not because his man had lost but because he had given a grave cause to Nehru to be angry with him." "At this stage", continues Mankekar, "I was called into the picture and asked to write the editorial on the victory. Goenka's strict instructions to me were to give the entire and exclusive credit for Krishna Menon's victory personally to Nehru, and deny any credit whatsoever to the Communists or even to Krishna Menon. I was told to emphasis Nehru's continued, unchallenged popularity with the Bombay voters in particular and the Indian people as a whole. Next morning Goenka flew to New Delhi and met Nehru, presented to him a copy of the Express drawing his attention to the edit. I have been told that he pleaded to Nehru that he believed in the freedom of the press and independence of the editor, a principle which Nehru himself had upheld. Goenka did not interfere with what his editor wrote. The implication was that the anti-Krishna Menon policy of the paper was entirely the handiwork of the editor."

It is obvious from what Mankekar has said that Goenka will swear by the freedom of the press when his calculations go wrong, and not when things happen in the other direction. When Krishna Menon won, inspite of his campaign, the blame for the campaign was laid at the door of the poor editor! If Kriplani had won, Goenka would have emerged as the sole claimant of the credit for defeating a Communist and saving Nehru from his hold!

III. He played the same role with Rajeev Gandhi when he sought to single out V.P.Singh for all the good things happened during Rajeev's tenure as Prime Minister

IV. The concept of freedom of the press implies a healthy distance from the political establishments. Those who seek to play the roles of adversaries or partisans, depanding upon the advantage accruing to their business interests, can never pass for the crusaders of the freedom of the press. This is because they can't remain objective and impartial once they get involved for their own stakes. In an affidavit filed by RNG before the Madras High Court, Goenka explained to the Court that the steps taken by the Government to prevent his taking-over the Indian Iron & Steel company were all designed to prevent him from exercising his fundamental freedom to run free newspapers! In other words, Goenka implied that the freedom of the press has the most important ingredient of the government helping newspaper barons to acquire the steel business, the cement business, the jute business and what not! What is the worth of freedom for a 'free' press if it does not help diversification in a variety of directions without bothering about the law and its restraints? This has been the recurring motive behind his hue and cry of "freedom of the press".

V. According to D.R. Mankekar, "if a poll were to be taken among the rank and file of journalist employees in the country to pick the most hated employers, Ramnath Goenka would win the title hands down".

The Vintagers of Goenka's Split vision

Ramnath Goenka's wife had expired on 1966 while his only son, Bhagwandas Goenka expired in 1979. Thus, his daughter Radha Bai Sonthalia and daughter-in-law, Saroj Goenka (the daughter of Sahu Shanti Prasad Jain's elder brother, the late Shreyans Prasad Jain) were the only solace to him. While B.D.Goenka was survived by his three daughters, Radha Sonthalia was blessed with three sons and three daughters. Her sons include Vivek, Manoj and Anil out of whom Vivek changed his surname from Sonthalia to Goenka consequent on his adoption as RNG's son. After Goenka's death, there was a prolonged legal battle fought by Saroj Goenka against Vivek Goenka and his associates, followed by yet another trail of suits initiated by Manoj Sonthalia, who was denied his due as the then Joint Managing Director of the group. As a result of Saroj Goenka's appeal to the Company Law Board and two cases filed by Manoj Sonthalia in the Madras High Court the Indian Express Empire witnessed a three-way partition of the company's assets. While the real estate had gone primarily to Saroj Goenka, the publishing business was carved into two - the financially strong northern editions (including the Bombay edition) were inherited by Vivek Goenka, the southern editions were given to Manoj Sothalia. The latter includes six southern editions of the Express now known as the "New Indian Express", Andhra Prabha (Telgu), Dinamani (Tamil), Cinema Express and Sterling group of magazines that also publishes 'Gentleman' from Bombay (sorry! Mumbai). Consequent on the partition, Sonthalia was required to shell out Rs.25 lakh a month for the premises at Chennai. According to one estimate, before partition the Express group had been sustaining a loss of Rs.36 crores per year on its printing business but the rentals it received from its 25 storey building in Mumbai's Nariman Point and certain other buildings elsewhere, compensated for the same. As on today, Vivek Goenka has nominal accommodation at Nariman Point and the bulk of the Bombay office has been shifted to a modest ground floor cottage type premises at Lal Bagh, the area that accommodated the defunct textile mills of Bombay where the local Shiv Sena becomes more vibrant during the Ganesh festival.

The Background of Conflict

The untimely death if B.D. Goenka, RNG's only son, gave rise to the apprehension that the widowed daughter-in-law (Saroj Goenka) would eventually wind-up the pulpdom of the Goenkas with a view to strengthening the monopoly of her parental family that owned "The Times of India' group of publications. This prompted the press baron to adopt Vivek as his son and to induct Manoj Sonthalia as one of the directors. After RNG's death, Vivek (who assumed the surname of RNG) took over as Managing Director while Manoj was designated the Joint Managing Director. This aggrieved Saroj Goenka who approached the Company Law Board as a petitioner. The petition was filed on 18.6.1993 under Sections 402, 408, 111, 235 and 250 of the Companies Act against M/s Nariman Point Building Services and Trading Pvt. and others.Shri R.C. Nag, counsel for the petitioner submitted that though the petitioners were not holding the required shares in the respondent company yet the petitioners were entitled to file the petition on the principle of doctrine of transfer of shares. The respondent companies were denying the membership of the petitioners. If the shares are transferred to the petitioners, the petitioners will be having one-third of the total shares in the respondent company which will be more than the required shareholding of 10% to present such petition. (The case was maintainable in terms of Supreme Court Judgment reported in AIR 1990 S.C. page 730). In a suit pending at Madras, the respondents had not disputed the 1/3 shareholding of the petitioners. According to the Counsel, the respondents had made some fraudulent entries in the share register. The petitioner was Managing director in one company but her powers were taken away. The respondents were fabricating the minute book. The Board (Principal Bench, New Delhi) issued an order on 25.6.1993 that restrained all the respondent companies from giving effect to any transfer or any transmission of shares in the said companies without prior leave of the Principal Bench. Besides, they were also restrained from increasing the issue and paid-up share capital in any manner as also from disposing of or encumbering their fixed assets or investments in any manner.

In the subsequent order dated 14.7.1993 it was directed that no respondent company in which petitioner no.1 was a director would hold Board meetings without giving at least three days' notice to the petitioner. While Saroj Goenka had approached the Company Law Board, it was Manoj Sonthalia who filed applications in a suit for a declaration that appointment of certain additional directors in the apex company was illegal, since he had no notice of the meeting at which they were appointed and that certain transfer of shares held by Manoj were invalid. Further, he sought a restoration of the power earlier enjoyed by him as a Joint Managing Director, claiming that the company had, step by step, stripped him of his powers and humiliated him, whereas the intention of the founder was that he and Vivek, the two grandsons of the founder should work as a team.

It was held that the Board of Directors in various resolutions had appointed Vivek Goenka as the executive director, managing editor and chairman, and it was not open to the court to interdict the functions of the board managed company; that Manoj Sonthalia had been accepting the appointment of the three additional directors by his own conduct by participating in several meetings with them, without objecting; that if Manoj Sonthalia's grievance was that this was a case of oppression of a minority by the majority, he had to move the appropriate forum constituted under the companies Act 1956. (Vivek Goenka v/s Manoj Sonthalia, April 13, 1993).

The climax of these disputes witnessed a three-way partition of Goenka's empire in which Saroj Goenka emerged as the real queen of real estate while Manoj Sonthalia inherited the southern editions out of blue (subsequently renamed as New-Express). Although Vivek Goenka emerged as Managing Director of Northern (including Bombay) editions, his sudden disappearance from India gave a new twist to the family drama. There were wider speculations in the market that perhaps he was secretly negotiating the sale or merger of his pulpdom wit that of mighty Murdoch's. This was repeatedly denied by Ananya Goenka, Vivek's wife. For almost 18 months Vivek was not available to anyone in India. The Grapevine has it that his prolonged stay abroad and frequent air-travels resulted in the form of a phobia of sorts for air-travel in general and 'air-hostesses' in particular. Perhaps the anti-climax is known to Mrs.Ananya Vivek Goenka. As on 01.03.2007, following is the list of shareholders holding more than one percent of the total capital of the Indian Express group (Mumbai) headed by Mr. Vivek Goenka:

I. M/s Indian Express Newspapers, (Mumbai) Ltd., Express Towers,   Nariman Point, Mumbai-400 021.

II. M/s. Nariman Point Building Services & Holdings Pvt. Ltd., Express   Towers, Nariman Point, Mumbai-400 021.

III. Mr. Viveck Goenka, Express Towers, Nariman Point, Mumbai-400 021.

IV. Mr. Shekhar Gupta, C-6/53, Safdarjang Development Area, New Delhi-110 016

5 The Mecca Of Hindi Journalism

Indore is considered the Mecca of Hindi journalism for different reasons to different persons. For those having academic interest in the evolution of Hindi journalism it is due to the late Rahul Barpute and his disciples who stream-lined the mainstream of cow-belt journalism at Bahadur Shah Zafar Marg in New Delhi. For others, it is either due to the vicinity of Mandsaur district that produces opium or the government land given to the press barons either free of cost or at a throw-away price, as a result of which the mushroom growth of the so-called press became inevitable. But primarily, the Indore syndrome can be understood as the culmination of the acts of omission and commission by the following Marwaris:

I. The late Labhchand Chhajlani alias "Babuji" of "Nai Duniya" who acquired the journal from the duo of Krishnakant Vyas and K.K.Mudgal.

II. The late Dwarka Das Agrawal of "Bhaskar" whose son Ramesh Chandra Agrawal happens to be the Chairman of the largest and fastest growing chain of Hindi newspapers published from 28 places.

III. The late Ram Gopal Maheshwari who founded, "Nav Bharat" & M.P. Chronicle.

The Success story of these three Marwaris triggered a chain reaction among all those whose inferiority complex compelled or misled them to acquire power at any cost. Under the circumstances, the mushroom growth of newspapers at Indore (and also at Bhopal) can be attributed to the following factors:

I.   The rivalry among Marwari press barons known for their "zero-budgeting";

II. The dependence of these Marwaris on politicians who in turn, had released substantial cash in the form of government advertisements;

III. The conflict between politicians and the press barons due to the inadequate or adverse coverage given to the former despite the generous gestures in the form of government advertisement;

IV. The press baron's megalomania that despite democracy, he alone is the "king-maker";

V.   The politician's dependence on criminals during elections in general and during "polling" in particular;

VI. The politician's dependence upon the press baron who withholds the news of electoral and post-electoral malpractices at a price.

The reconciliation between the politician and the press baron in "cash or kind" further strengthens the mafia of criminals who are invariably linked with smugglers, foreign mercenaries, drug-paddlers and terrorists. Needless to say, the major beneficiaries in the entire process are criminals and foreign intelligence agencies whose remote control over the press barons and politicians can hardly be over-emphasized.

The Mandsaur Factor

Another factor that focused Indore on the intelligence map of the pre-globalized world was its vicinity to Mandsaur (the district that produces opium). The nexus between opium cultivators and the politicians cannot be ruled out. At the same time, the politicians contesting from the opium constituency or its vicinity are fully dependent upon the support of the newspaper in the area that has a substantial circulation. This has facilitated the convoluted network of criminals who exploit the situation on reciprocal basis. Thus, unpredictable politicians, holy press barons & covert smugglers/white ravens are hand in glove as elaborated in the following hypothetical example:

"Suppose a political party called PP-1 needs financial donations to conduct the imminent general elections in the State. Let us also suppose that PP-1 is in power not only in M.P. but also in Maharashtra and at the Centre. Now, if a smuggler called Bhai-one (B-1) proposes to give a donation of Rs. One crore subject to the condition that his truck containing opium products will not be obstructed anywhere from Mandsaur to Bombay and from the city of Bombay to the port where the actual shipment should be allowed without questioning. Now, suppose that the party boss agrees to the proposal of the B-1 and instructs the political incumbents at New Delhi, Bhopal and Bombay to facilitate the same. So far, things are going smoothly but all of a sudden, a press baron called PB-1 comes to know the secret. Now the success of his operation depends upon a seven letter word called "setting" which has different meanings for different parties but an un-equivocal one for the one who is sued for defamation in the Court of Law. It is here that we make a mockery of freedom and allow "Mr. Criminal" to go scot-free. As a result, the Bhai operates even when he does not donate to the political party because he has thoroughly understood the modus-operandi and the personators. In fact, he is able to operate at reduced cost because, after elections, every personator is scared of the other. Occasionally, the lack of co-ordination is reflected in the media either in the form of condemnation of the Police or that of the smuggler turned-politician, who at times, resolves the situation by launching a tabloid of his own. Once tabloid or its broadsheet avatar is launched, pimps, prostitutes, politicians and power brokers are all praise for the new press baron.

Perhaps the above hypothesis can be formulated as follows:

I. The prosperity (PRO) of a smuggler (or criminal) called B1 is directly proportional to the quantum of donation (read bribe) given to the politician called P1 provided the Ruling Party in question continues to remain in power.

$$\textbf{PRO.B1} \propto \textbf{P1}$$

$$[\propto = \text{Sign of proportionality}]$$

In order to change the sign of proportionality($\propto$) into the sign of equality (=) we need a constant, which happens to be the Ruling Party concerned in this case. Thus given the benefit of **K** (constant),

$$\textbf{PRO.B1.K} = \textbf{P1}$$

Under different circumstances **PRO.B1** could also change as more than or less than that of the politician:

$$\textbf{PRO.B1} > \textbf{P1}$$

or

$$\textbf{PRO.B1} < \textbf{P1}$$

In critical situations, the relationship can be inversely proportional which should not surprise the students of media management.

II. Similarly, the prosperity of a press baron called **B1** is directly proportional to the number of illegal transactions (read crimes) which either remain un-reported (UR) in his journal or the coverage of which is withheld for a price to be negotiated, provided the criminals involved in the transaction including their supporters do not own any newspaper in the state.

Thus,

$$\textbf{PRO.B1} \propto \textbf{CR.UR}$$

[UR = crime un-reported]

Here also, the sign of proportionality can be changed into the sign of equality with the help of a constant (**K**), which stands for the number of newspapers in this case. In other words if the number of newspapers published from a particular state or city is constant than the above equation can be changed as follows:

$$\textbf{PRO.B1} = \textbf{CR.UR}$$

Incidentally, this may be clarified that the term crime used in this hypothesis not only includes the acts of omission and commission already covered under IPC and Cr.P.C. but also the following:

i. Any act that spreads journacracy in the name of journalism thereby weakening the democratic set-up and the constitutional authority of the Executive, Legislative and Judicial wings of the government;

ii. Any act that promotes or aims at promoting any criminal as a hero or messiah of public cause;

iii. any overt or overt act of publishing advertisement as a news item;

iv. Any act or attempt of obtaining a monopoly position for self or an associate or family kin of the press baron in the realm of commercial supply of requisite commodities to the Municipal Corporation or a public sector organization due mainly to the influence of the newspaper;

v. To act as broker in the realm of purchase of diamonds or precious stones especially when such stones are used as a mode of payment of astronomical sums to a politician or a mafia don;

vi. Any act on the part of the press baron intended to control any charitable/religious trust through self, associates or family kins especially when the trust in question has huge resources in cash, kind or real estate;

vii. Any act or intention of withholding a news item that may render more cash or real value than publishing the same under "classified" or "display" category of advertisements;

viii. To accept any government land or property at throwway price with an implied consent to give media coverage to the politician who is instrumental in such an allotment;

ix. Any act or attempt that aims at obtaining exemption from income tax/entertainment tax for any event organized or sponsored by the newspaper or its associates;

x. Any act or attempt to launch a banking or non-banking financial company such as a plantation company, in the name of the press baron or his family members or associates or distant kins;

xi. Any act or intervention between a public sector bank and its borrower that may result in the waiver or non-payment of debt due to political influence of the newspaper;

xii. Any act of lobbying for a high profile post in government sector such as membership of Public Service Commission or head honcho's position in the State Finance Corporation for the press baron's family members or business associates or distant cousins or concubines;

xiii. Any nexus with criminals, smugglers, mafia-dons, land grabbers or white collar dacoits against whom almost every newspaper writes an editorial or two every week.

The above list is only illustrative and not exhaustive.

The Marwari Funda

Whatever be the hidden reasons behind the ever-increasing numerical strength of Hindi broadsheets and tabloids in Malwa, the lifeline that sustains their financial viability is the Marwari technique of financial management which is more clandestine than what is reflected in the double entry system of accounting. Needless to say, the present generation of Malwa based *banias* is a genetic continuity of descendents of those migrants from Rajasthan who had emigrated to this coveted land in search of fodder for their cattle and mulah for themselves. The non-Marwari media enterprisers in the present day Malva/M.P. are either ex-employees of the Marwari or their tax-consultants. Before we venture to understand the genetically inherited Marwari technique of financial management, it is desirable to know the ethnic groups that constitute the Marwari conglomerate.

"Marwari" is a package term for four communities of Rajasthani origin viz; Agrawals, Maheswaris, Saravagis and Oswals. The Saravagis and Oswals are also jointly known as Jains. Whether it is the TOI of Sameer Jain or Hindustan Times of Birlas or the Indian Express of Goenka or the fastest growing Bhaskar Group of Ramesh Agrawal or the Nava Bharat Group of Maheswaris or the historic Nai Dunia of Chhajlanis or the DNA of Agrawals and Goels, the fact remains that all these newspapers belong to one Marwari or the other.

Marwari is genetically programmed to mint money irrespective of his ignorance of the technology implied in the end-product that he sells. Despite globalization, the community continues to own more than 80% of the Indian gold reserves in some form or the other. What concerns an average Indian is not the quantity of gold held by a particular community but the bend of mind that first monopolizes resources, institutions and opportunities, and then inflicts suffering on fellow human beings by rendering them helpless. In the realm of media management, the proprietor has an additional advantage! First he obstructs the vision by prescribing blinkers and then sells his subscribers/readers/viewers as commodities to the advertisers of which the victims are hardly aware.

While all the press barons cannot be blamed for the ruthless exploitation of their employees and almost ubiquitous tendency to blackmail against the "withheld" news, it would be equally unjust to include or exclude only the Marwari ones for such a condemnation. The fact remains that these power-drunk entities cannot be condemned or condoned in a democracy! There are exceptions like the late G.D, Birla who fuelled the flame of the freedom movement by funding the Hindustan Times; Mr. Vijaypat Singhania, who stopped the publication of 'Indian Post' on moral grounds and the least known but profoundly sensitive enterpriser, Mr. Kamal Morarka who rescued Mr. Behram Contractor from the claws of the "spectre" that used to haunt the Mid Day premises. Due credit should also be given to Mrs. Rama Jain, the daughter of Mr. R. K. Dalmia and the grandma of Mr. Sameer Jain. Although eyebrows were raised against Mr. K.K.Birla when he sacked Mr. B.G.Verghese in the early seventies and Mr. Khushwant Singh in the early eighties of the preceding century, this is nothing as compared to R.N.-Goenka's record who had sacked Mr. Arun Shourie thrice. Incidentally, this also speaks volumes about Mr. Shourie's self respect. As regards Mr. Khushwant Singh, he has already begged a column in the same newspaper that had unceremoniously settled his accounts at the reception counter.

The Marwari Strategy

While it is almost impossible to render the Marwari strategy of financial management in words, an approximate account may be presented by someone who was either victimized by the Marwari or has been serving the Marwari employer as his *Muneem* or Accountant. Perhaps no Marwari would forgive me for the following generalizations:

As a thumb rule, the Marwari is unrivalled in the art of converting public money into private money. Hence, he is exclusively privileged to launch a newspaper without any investment from his own pocket. This involves a two pronged strategy -

I. To procure land and machinery either on credit or by taking-over a running unit for which he is reluctant to pay in cash unless the commodity is available at a throw-away price such as Rs. 200/- against the market price of Rs. 2,000/-. The act of taking-over involves a convoluted mechanism in which the Marwari joins the running unit either as a partner or promoter or as a broker of some financer. In both the cases, either he pays a paltry sum from somebody else's pocket or procures "invisibles" on his credit and never forgets to promise the moon to all concerned. In a vulnerable State like Madhya Pradesh, there is a soft option tailor-made for the Marwari. Land is allotted by the Government on lease or at nominal rates. Loan is facilitated through the State finance corporation/nationalized banks for the construction of office building/ purchase of plant and machinery. After initial payment of a few installments this loan becomes a bad debt either due to change of partners or liquidation of the original unit or disappearance of plant and machinery or morphing of ABC Company into XYZ Company or sale of the unit by someone who is already dead. Eventually, the loans written off due mainly to a political nexus.

II. For human resources, the Marwari swings into action only after he has taken-over the management. While petty cash payments are honoured after postponed intervals, those demanding four-figure amounts are advised to contact the predecessor. After thorough scrutiny for retrenchment, the staff is reduced to one-fourth of the existing strength. This is followed by the induction of three persons of Mr. Marwari's choice. The first and foremost is the chief accountant or the financial controller who is promised partnership in the future. However, the extent of the proposed partnership depends upon the incumbent's capacity to reduce the astronomical sums of the Profit and Loss Account into algebraic ones. For reasons known to the Chartered Accountants, this man is retained in the organization till he breathes his last even if he has been rendered "immobile" by disease or a "pre-planned" attack. The other incumbent being the Chief Executive, who is the highest paid factotum of the organization. Next, in the hierarchy is the chief editor whose salary depends upon the following factors:

   (i) The extent to which he can boost the newspaper's circulation

   (ii) His capacity to goad youngsters as apprentices for reporting or editorial assignments on a shoe-string remuneration or no remuneration

Where the Marwari faces stiff competition with market leaders, he picks up technically qualified personnel on higher remuneration from his rival's establishment. This can be illustrated as follows:

If a technocrat is getting a salary of Rs.60,000/- p.m. in the organization which is No.1 in the area, the Marwari will pick him for Rs.80,000/- p.m. His (the Marwari's) Man Friday would work as an Assistant under this new incumbent on a monthly salary of Rs.6,000/- p.m. After six months, the Man Friday emerges as a trained personnel. Now the Marwari tells the technocrat that due to this or that reason, he would not be in a position to pay him more than Rs. 30,000/- as salary. Obviously, the technocrat can't go back to his original employer. If he quits, the Marwari gives an increment of Rs.4,000/- to his Man Friday and promotes him in place of the outgoing technocrat. Thus, he gets a technically qualified person for Rs.10,000/- p.m. for which the market leader is paying Rs.60,000/- p.m.

It is in the background of this strategy that the ethnic pattern of the editorial incumbent emerges. My prolonged observations have revealed that no Marwari can boost the circulation of a Hindi daily without involving a Kanyakubja or a Kayasth as editor in the initial stage. If the journal is an English daily, the editorial entity is either a Bengali or a South Indian. After the circulation is stabilized at a certain level, the editorial incumbent is replaced by the press baron's son or by a smart Punjabi chap who gives more coverage to the itsy-bitsy bikini and the erotic art of removing hair from the soft tissues.

When Pandit Ambika Prasad Vajpeyee launched a Hindi daily before Independence, he could not run it beyond six months. As a result, his own Marwari employee purchased the press and the newspaper from him at a throw-away price. The name of this Marwari was Mulchand Agrawal. However, the Marwari launched a new journal called 'Vishvamitra' which became a roaring success. Impressed by the success, when his friend Prabhu Dayalu Agnihotri wanted to know the secret, the Marwari revealed the following sutras[22]:

---

[22] 'Akshara' published by M.P.Rashtra Bhasha Prachar Samity, Bhopal (November-December 2005 Issue)

(i) Only a "non-entity' without any market value should
be appointed as the editor.

(ii) The editor should not hold any academic degree that
may enable   him to apply elsewhere.

(iii) As far as possible, only Brahmins should be employed in the editorial department. If the proprietor
touches the feet of these Brahmins, they would be grati-
fied to work at a scanty salary or   practically without
salary for the extra work that they render.

(iv) No 'Baniya' (a person belonging to the mercantile
community such as the Marwari employer himself)
should be appointed in the Advertisement Department,
the reason being, such a person's   potential to de-
velop personal relations with the advertisers, ultimately
enabling him to launch his own journal with the help of
his employer's advertisers.

(v) Every member of the editorial staff should be asked to
originate at least five columns of matter to qualify for
that day's remuneration.

(vi) Don't terminate any member of the editorial staff. Instead, give him one or two months' salary in advance
and ask him to take rest for a while with an assurance
that he would be welcomed as and when he feels like
joining. This would prevent strikes and lock-outs.

Incidentally, it may be clarified that the above sutras are
not exhaustive but only illustrative. For a detailed study of
Marwari sutras, one should either read their biographies or
share the experience of ex-partners, ex-employees and
Chartered Accountants associated with them.

6 The Evolution Of Nai Duniya

As stated earlier, the journal was founded by the Brahmanical duo of K.K. Vyas and K.C. Mudgal but was subsequently acquired by the late Babu Labhchand Chhajlani alias Babujee. Although this fact has been mentioned umpteen times in the books devoted to the history of Hindi journalism in M.P., it was never clarified whether any amount was paid for the transfer of ownership or it was only against the adjustment of assets and liabilities? The first authentic account of this 'acquisition' has been reported by Shri Jawahar Lal Rathore who was an active stringer and distributing agent of the journal at Jhabua:

इंदौर में दैनिक नई दुनिया का प्रकाशन 5 जून 1947 से प्रारंभ हुआ।पंडित कृष्णकांत व्यास उसके संपादक और श्री कृष्णचंद मुदगल प्रकाशक थे। व्यासजी, प्रजामंडल पत्रिका का पहले ही संपादन कर रहे थे...अगस्त 1947 में 'नई दुनिया' एक सायंकालीन सात कालम का अखबार था। न्यूज़प्रिंट पर नहीं, अलग-अलग प्रकार के कागजों पर भार्गव फाइन आर्ट्स प्रेस पर छपता था। छपाई आकर्षक नहीं थी। ग़लतियां भी छपाई में काफी रहती थीं। उसकी स्पर्धा मुख्यत: 'इंदौर समाचार' से थी।दोनों में तगड़ी स्पर्धा चलती थी। नवंबर,1947 तक नई दुनिया भारी आर्थिक संकट में फंस गया था। प्रकाशक, श्री कृष्णचंद्र मुदगल असंतुष्ट हो, 'नई दुनिया' छोड़ गए थे। प्रधान संपादक श्री कृष्णकांत व्यास ने 'नई दुनिया' के प्रकाशन और

प्रबंधन में बाबू लाभचंद छजलानी को शामिल किया। उन्होंने श्री बसंतीलाल सेठिया और श्री नत्थूलाल तिवारी (बाद में नाम हुआ नरेंद्र तिवारी) को अपने साथ जोड़ा। एक नई टीम बनी। दिसंबर,1947 में माडर्न प्रिंटरी (प्रा) लिमिटेड के कड़ावघाट स्थित प्रेस में 'नई दुनिया' का संपादन, मुद्रण, प्रकाशन प्रारंभ हुआ।सभी एजेंसियों की समीक्षा की गई और सबके हिसाब-किताब व्यवस्थित किए गए।"

Free Translation: "The Publication of *Nai Duniya* commenced at Indore from 5th of June 1947. Pandit K.K.Vyas was its chief editor, while K.C. Mudgal was the publisher. Vyasji was already editing Prajamandal Partika at that time ... In August 1947 *Nai Duniya* was an eveninger of seven columns. It was not published on newsprint, but on different varieties of paper, at The Bhargava Arts press. The printing was not attractive as it had innumerable errors. Its main competitor was 'Indore Samachar'. There was a neck-to-neck competition between the two. By November 1947, *Nai Duniya* witnessed the worst financial crisis. Shri K.C.-Mudgal, the publisher was so much disgruntled that he withdrew from the set-up. Shri K.K. Vyas inducted Babu Labhchand Chhajlani for the publication and management of the journal who in turn, inducted Shri Basantilal Sethia and Shri Natthulal Tiwari (who subsequently changed his name and became Narendra Tiwari) in the new team. It was during December 1947 that the editing, printing and publication of *Nai Duniya* was started at Modern Printery Pvt. Ltd. The arrangements with all the agencies were renewed and the accounts were streamlined.[23]

It appears that Shri K.K. Vyas continued to be the de-jure editor till 1951 despite Babu Labhchand Chhajlani's induc-

---

[23] ***Smriti Bimb*** (Hindi) page 123 published and edited by Vijay Datta Shridhar for Mahadev Rao Sapre Sangrahalaya Bhopal (June 2000).

tion at the helm of affairs, as is clear from the following account rendered by the same stringer:

" **मध्य भारत** राज्य का निर्माण तो 28 मई,1948 को हो चुका था किंतु पत्रकार प्रादेशिक स्तर पर असंगठित रहे। पहली बार मध्य- भारत में श्रमजीवी पत्रकारों का सम्मेलन इंदौर के गांधी हाल में नवम्बर,1951में हुआ। उसके स्वागताध्यक्ष थे नई दुनिया के प्रधान संपादक, पंडित कृष्णकांत व्यास। सम्मेलन की अध्यक्षता की थी पंडित बालकृष्ण शर्मा "नवीन" ने।

Free Translation: "The state of Madhya Pradesh was constituted on 28th of May 1948 but the journalists remained un-organised at the state-level. The first ever conference of the working journalists of Madhya Pradesh was held at Gandhi Hall of Indore during November 1951. Pandit K.K.Vyas, the chief editor of Nai Duniya headed the reception committee while Pandit B.K. Sharma 'Naveen' presided."

Indore and the adjoining geographical area from Mandsaur to Sehore (say Bhopal) is traditionally known as Malwa. Before independence it was ruled by the Scindias of Gwalior whose kingdom extended from Gwalior to Mandsaur via Ujjain. However, Indore was ruled by the Holkars and the rivalry between Scindias and Holkars had assumed mythological proportions before independence. As per past records, Rajasthan had been and to some extent continues to be, a drought-prone area. This constrained the habitants of all hues and colours to migrate to the green pastures of Malwa in search of dal-roti if not bread and butter. Since the population of Malwa was predominantly tribal and illiterate, Marwaris found it convenient to prosper un-opposed. As a result, Marwari banias continued to settle in Malwa with the original asset of a lota-dori. The list included luminaries like the legendary Sir Seth Hukum Chand whose Lota-dori is still pawned for Rupee one at Indore.

The Chhajlanis were lucky enough to have settled at Indore without pawning any lota-dori as they had reached the city via Banaras where they had emigrated from a small village in the BIAVAR district of Rajasthan. It was at Banaras that the Chhajlanis were over-shadowed by the convoluted Kanya-Kubjas, power sharing Lalas, dubious jugglers and the beguiling tantriks all of whom had an edge over the usufruct Marwaris. In 1922, they landed on the soil of Indore as recorded on the edit-page of Nai Duniya dated 20.1.1981:

"देश के आजाद होने के बाद 1947 की अंतिम तिमाही में उन्होंने श्री कृष्णकांत व्यास से यह समाचारपत्र ले लिया जो उसे चला नहीं पा रहे थे। जन्म बनारस में 31 जुलाई 1909 को।1922 में वे इंदौर आए।उनके पिता श्री हरकचंद छजलानी जौहरी थे और हीरे-जवाहरात के मामले में वे होलकरों के सलाहकार रहे। शुरू में बाबूजी ने बहुत कम वेतन पर नौकरी की और लगभग उन्हीं दिनों स्वाधीनता के सिलसिले में कांग्रेस और प्रजा मंडल की गतिविधियों में दिलचस्पी लेने लगे।इसी कारण उन्हें यह नौकरी गंवाना पड़ी जो उनकी आजीविका का मुख्य स्रोत थी।"

Free Translation: " After independence, he took-over this newspaper in the last quarter of 1947 from Shri K.K. Vyas who was not able to run it. He was born on 31st of July 1909 at Banaras. He arrived at Indore in 1922. His father Harakchandji Chhajlani was a jeweler who also worked as a connoisseur of diamonds to the Holkars. In the beginning, Babujee undertook a job for a very scanty salary and it was during this period that he associated himself with the activities of the Congress and *Prijamandal* in connection with the freedom movement. It was due to these activities that he lost his job which was the main source of his livelihood".

On the occasion of his funeral at Dewas Ghat Crematorium of Indore, Shri Babulal Patodi had stated, "बाबूजी ने इस शहर में राजकुमार मिल में एक निष्ठावान सेवक के रूप में अपना जीवन प्रारंभ

किया " (Babujee had started his life as a faithful servant in the Rajkumar Mill of this city). Perhaps this is a reference to a blue-collar job that he had accepted at the Rajkumar Mills. The Grapevine has it that Babujee also worked as an assistant to the dealer who handled *satta* transactions in the realm of speculative bids. The historic spot is presently situated behind the famous *Rajwada* of Indore where it is predominantly occupied by the *Sindhi* monopolists of readymade garments. The fact that he had launched and developed the newspaper without any investments of his own, was corroborated in the editiorial of *Nai Duniya* dated 20.2.1998 as follows:

"जब 1961 में माडर्न प्रिंटरी के संचालकत्व से हटने के बाद वे नई दुनिया का दफ्तर किबे- कंपाउंड में ले गए और मशीन वगैरह का सारा इंतजाम उन्हें नए सिरे से करना पड़ा...बड़ी थैली के बगैर आज कोई अच्छा अख़बार निकालने की कल्पना भी नहीं कर सकता लेकिन सिर्फ़ बीस साल पहले अपनी अपराजेयता और वफादार साथियों की एक टीम के बूते पर लाभचंद जी ने लगभग बिना पैसे के एक अख़बार खड़ा कर दिया और यह सिद्ध किया कि कभी-कभी सार्वजनिक ऋण से भी समाज में ऐसी संस्थाएं खड़ी हो सकती हैं जो अपने अंचल में सांस्कृतिक परिचय-चिन्ह बन जाएं।"

Free Translation: "After he dis-associated himself with the Modern Printery as one of its directors he shifted the office of *Nai Duniya* to Kibey Compound and once again, he had to arrange machine and everything from scratch. Now-a-days, nobody can even imagine that a good newspaper can be launched without substantial investment. But it was barely 20 years ago, that Labhchandjee had materialized a newspaper on the strength of his own invulnerability and a team of faithful associates, particularly without any mone-tary investment and proved that even Public debt can help materialize such institutions which may eventually emerge as cultural icons in the regions."

At this stage, perhaps it is desirable to know as to how and why Babujee first joined or goaded Modern Printery and why was he constrained to withdraw therefrom? As recorded by J.L. Rathore, "*Nai Duniya* resumed its publication at the Modern Printery in December 1947". In fact, Babujee had nailed a peg long before he ordered his "Coat". For this we shall have to dig the past of all those whose presence prompted Babujee to visualize the *grand finale*, an event, which would have remained a dream had he not met Mr. Basantilal Sethia alias, 'Bhaiyaji' and Mr. Bal Krishna Shah of Siyaganj who was nicknamed by Marwaris as 'Gandya Bhai'.

In conformity with the Marwari tradition of "free gains", both Babujee and Babujee used to visit a newspaper vendor's shop at Indore where they could read all the newspapers without requiring to pay a single penny. However, the bond of friendship was strengthened during World War II when Bhaiyaji worked as a broker in the local Stock Market and needed a radio-set to apprise himself of the activities affecting the market. This constrained him to visit the joint family establishment of Chhajlanis who owned a radio-set. Babujee's eldest brother, Umrao Chand was alive at that time and had already distinguished himself as a diamond-setter. During the Quit India Movement both Babujee and Bhaiyaji remained in the same jail and that strengthened the bond further. As soon as Babujee was relieved from the jail in November 1934, he launched a small printing unit where Bhaiyaji also approached him for a job. This inspired Babujee to visualize a bigger unit where like-minded persons could be exploited for a common cause. In 1946 he prompted Balkrishna Shah to launch a private limited company that could handle printing and publication on a large scale. By that time, Babuji had already joined him (Mr.

Shah) as an assistant in the realm of general insurance. While a major investment was effected by Mr. B.K. Shah and his associates, Babujee and Mr. Kamla Shankar Pandya had also purchased shares that subsequently enabled them to become directors.

It was on Babujee's advice that Bhaiyaji also purchased shares of Modern Printery, issued on the first of July 1946. Babujee entered into a long term agreement with Balkrishna Shah at a 'Fixed rate' that enabled him not only to get the paper printed on credit but also much below the prevailing market rates. As Gujaratis are considered to be 'lesser usufructs' than Marwaris, Mr. Shah found it a lucrative business for Modern Printery. But he failed to realize that he was providing infrastructural facilities to Babujee at a shoe-string budget. While all the labour problems, wages, energy bills, wear and tear were to be borne by the Modern Printery, *Nai Duniya* would settle the previous months bill at its own convenience after recovering the revenue from its agents, advertisers and distributors, to say nothing about "invisibles". Despite all this, if there were any distant hopes of profit, Babujee and his associates would be sharing the same not only in the form of directors' dues but also as dividends to which all the share-holders were entitled.

Meanwhile, Babujee appointed Bhaiyaji as a 'two-in-one' Accountant for both, Modern Printery and *Nai Duniya* in December 1948. (What they don't teach you at Harward). Balkrishna Shah learnt his first lesson from the Marwari mentor when he realized after sometime that his entire staff and resources at the Modern Printery were being utilized for Nai Duniya's gain and that the pulp-whore was eating into the vitals of his investments. But he was already "fettered" as the agreement made it obligatory on the part of Modern Printery to print the paper at the mutually agreed rate for the mutually agreed period. So, it was a great relief to the Gujrati speaking Directors of Modern Printery when they ultimately got rid of the Marwari stranglehold. But they had to pay a very heavy price for the same. All their financial resources remained locked for 14 long years only to pave the way for betterment of a Marwari who used them as financial condoms.

When Babujee separated from Modern Printery in January 1961, he shifted the office of *Nai Duniya* to Kibe Compound in the rented premises owned by Mr. Mohan Lunkad. Mr. Mohan Lunkad was one of the two sons of M/s Sagarmal Nathmal of Jalgaon who along with his other brother, was a leading cine-distributer of his time. Their firm, 'Vasant Pictures' was known to all the press barons of Western - India for the cine-advertisements that they released. Lunkads being Marwaris, themselves, knew that they had nothing to lose as the dues, if any, could be bartered against the bills of advertisements that they released. Once premises were acquired, the immediate problem of Babujee was to procure machinery for the printing unit for which he had no money. Babujee, along with Mr. Narendra Tiwari (whose name appeared as the Managing Director) approached a bureaucrat at New Delhi who had also worked as Chief Secretary in the Liliput of Madhya Bharat during the olden golden period of Babujee's innings as a King-maker. It was due mainly to the good offices of this bureaucrat that Babujee and Tiwariji met Mr. Anand Rao Surana (again a Marwari) who owned Indo-Europa, a firm that used to import printing-press units for its clients in India. Once of the daughters of the Surana family was already a daughter-in-law in the Thakuriya family of Indore who owned the then Prakash Talkies in the city. All said and done, Suranas obliged Babujee with a Polygraph Printing Machine on credit. Subsequently, when Nai-Duniya required more sophisticated machinery, Babujee approached Mr. Lal Chand Sethi, the then Deputy Chairman of the M.P.Finance Corporation. Originally, Mr. Sethi was an industrialist who owned the famous Vinod Mills at Ujjain. Since Mr. Sethi was also a Jain, the possibility of Babujee's lobbying for his nomination to the high profile post of the M.P.Finance Corporation cannot be ruled out. Mr. Sethi promptly sanctioned Babujee's loan proposal. As per rules, only 75% of the total cost of the machinery could be sanctioned. When Babujee drew a blank face for the margin money, Mr. Sethi rose to the occasion by drawing a cheque from his own cheque book.

Babujee never felt happy at the rented premises and waited for an opportunity that could make him a landlord. It was during 1964 or so that the last monarch of Indore breathed his last. There were two claimants to the notional throne, real estate and the strings that controlled the privy-purse. Destiny appeared to be destined to bless Babujee who had supported the cause of Princess Usha, the daughter of the deceased ruler. For reasons known to the trustees and beneficiaries of the Princess Usha Trust as also to the then city reporter of Nai-Duniya, the paper was awarded prime land at a notional price in the vicinity of the Lal Bagh Palace, where it continues to hold its main office together with the residential bungalow that Babujee had built for his offsprings. The area was known as Kesar Bagh Road which was renamed Babu Labhchand Chhajlani Marg after Babujee breathed his last in January 1981. It was at Kesar Bagh Road that Babujee created history in the cow-belt journacracy by importing and installing the first off-set printing unit that any Hindi journal could boast of. Here again, Babujee was lucky as he had saved 36% amount on the prevailing price of the machine as the Indian Rupee was devalued by 36% on 06-06-1966 and Babujee had placed his order before that date.

Now *Nai Duniya* had its own premises, its own sophisticated machinery and buildings in the offing. The open space was used as a nursery to promote the sale of plants, saplings and "potential flowers". As on that date, *Nai Duniya* had three partners:

I. Babuji alias Babu Labhchand Chhajlani, who owned 60% shares;

II. Shri Narendra Tiwari, the Managing Editor, who held 20% shares; and

III. Bhaiyaji alias Basantialal Sethia, who held 20% shares.

Although, Bhaiyaji and Tiwariji were partners, they were not allotted any chunk of land in the newly acquired premises. Nor did they suspect anything fishy in the convoluted wisdom of their mentor who had materialized three dimensional assets out of the never visible fourth dimension. Before the linguistic re-organization of Indian States in 1956, Babujee had already established his credentials as a 'King maker' of sorts in the erstwhile Madhya Bharat state whose capital was shared by Indore and Gwalior. The late Leeladhar Joshi was the first Chief Minister of the Madhya Bharat state. He was the descendant of the original Brahmin rulers of Indore from whom the *Marathas* had taken-over. He was succeeded by Mr. Gopi Krishna Vijayvargiya, followed by Mr. Takhatmal Jain and Mr. Mishrilal Gangwal (Jain) in quick succession. At the time of re-organization of States, once again, Mr. Takhatmal Jain was in the CM's saddle. Both Babu Takhatmal Jain and Mr. Mishrilal Gangwal considered Babujee as their political mentor. But alas! They had nothing to offer as *gurudakshina* to the mentor except the government advertisements, which they did release to the hilt. On the first of November 1956, the new state of Madhya Pradesh was constituted in which the old Madhya Bharat state was also merged. Pandi Ravi Shankar Shukla (the father of Emergency fame Vidya Charan Shukla), was the first Chief Minister of this newly constituted State. He had already ruled the old state of Madhya Pradesh that excluded Madhya Bharat but included the Vidarbha area of the present day Maharashtra. It was in the old Madhya Pradesh that Pandit Dwarka Prasad Mishra was the Home Minister in the cabinet of Pandit Ravi Shankar Shukla at Nagpur.

Since Pandit Ravi Shankar Shukla ws facing charges of corruption, Pandit Nehru denied him an election ticket that could renew his Chief Ministership. This caused a massive heart attack and Pandit Shukla was consigned to the dustbin of history. Nehru wanted an honest and obedient Chief Minister for the newly constituted State that had the largest geographical area in the country. His natural choice fell on Kailash Nath Katzu, a Kashmiri-Brahmin who was born at Jaora in MP where his father was Prime Minister in the erstwhile Jaora State, ruled by a Nawab till 1947. Katzu being an honest man, was naïve in politics. His only strength was Nehru's support. This curtailed the stature of Babujee as a Kingmaker for the 'king' was imposed by Nehru and Babujee was no match to the dazzling aura of Pandit Jawaharlal Nehru. Nevertheless, Babujee continued to meddle in the politics of Madhya Pradesh through his puppets and the pulpdom. He had no problem with Katzu as the latter was amenable to media promptings and Babujee's protege, Shri Mishrilal Gangwal was already enjoying the number two position (perhaps as Finance Minister) in Katzu's cabinet. But the State of Madhya Pradesh was not a replica of

Madhya Bharat as the *Kanyakubja* lobby spearheaded by Pandit D.P.Mishra had worked overtime to carve out a State that could settle political scores with Pandit Nehru (who had expelled Mishrajee from the Congress Party for six long years). It was Pandit Mishra's cherished dream to succeeed Nehru as the Prime Minister for which he needed the support of the majority of M.Ps. (Members of Parliament). Since U.P. had the largest No. of Parliamentary constituencies in the country, Pandit Mishra visualized a state that could outnumber the same. He got an opportunity to do so as a member of the Commission that recommended the linguistic re-organization of Indian States. When this was finalized in 1956, Nehru was flabbergasted at the advent of the gigantic size of Madhya Pradesh but he was clueless to the genesis that conceived a nemesis. Pandit Mishra was confident that sooner or later he should be in-charge of the Congress party in Madhya Pradesh where he would distribute election tickets to his favourites who, in turn, would support him for Prime Ministership after Nehru.

Perhaps Pandit Mishra was living in a fool's paradise but the *Kanyakubja* lobby was aware that as a Home Minister in Pandit Shukla's cabinet, Mishraji was in constant touch with Sardar Vallabhbhai patel. The reason was simple the top leadership of the R.S.S. was detained in The Nagpur Central Jail after Mahatma Gandhi's assassination in 1948. Being an old associate of Patel, he had already witnessed the nitty-gritty of rescuing India from the clutches of those descendants of the Semitic invaders who had shamelessly declared their intention to join Pakistan. Pandit Mishsra was also aware that the Congress Party had elected Patel to be the Prime Minister (it was only at Mahatma Gandhi's intervention that Nehru was assigned Prime-Ministership and Patel was persuated to accept him as the leader). It was in the light of this background that Mishraji considered himself not only as the successor to Nehru but also as a true successor to Vallabhbhai Patel. In the parlance of cow-belt slang, he was a *Kanyakubja*, "who controlled all the thirteen kitchens of the joint family". In the heart of hearts, he identified himself with the legendary Kautilya of *Arthashastra* fame.

While the MLAs of the old Madhya Bharat region of Madhya Pradesh were following the edicts of Babujee, those belonging to the Mahakaushal and Vindhya region had formed a beeline behind Pandit D.P.Mishra who had completed six years of his political exile. Mrs.Indira Gandhi was the President of the Congress Party at that time and Nehru had already turned mild and depressed due to the Chinese attack on India. It was the most appropriate occasion for Pandit D.P. Mishra to return to the Congress fold. As luck would have it, Uma Shankar Deekshit, another Kanyakubja (the father-in-law of Sheela Deekshit), introduced him to Indiraji who not only okayed his re-entry into the Congress, but also, allowed him to contest as an MLA on the Congress ticket. Meanwhile, Bhagvant Rao Mandloi of Khandwa succeeded Katzu for a short period pending D.P.Mishra's triumphant victory as the fourth Chief Minister of Madhya Pradesh.

Being a hardcore Marwari, the only forte of Babujee was credit management. This prevented him from developing any serious reading habits as his prime time was consumed in the financial management of 'transferred caps'. He was not aware of Pandit Mishra's political profile. Moreover, he was power-drunk and had a conviction that anybody who wanted to rule Madhya Pradesh would have to seek his patronage as Indore was the hub center of industrial production that streamlined the quantum of donation to political parties. All said and done, Babujee was not aware that Pandit D.P. Mishra was a *Kanyakubja Shiromani* who had already ruled the erstwhile Sagar Varsity as a sovereign. Perhaps it was the only varsity in MP where the majority of staff consisted of Pandit Mishra's community of *Kanyakubja* Brahmins. Perhaps Babujee had no idea of the *Kanyakubja* brand of Brahmins and their self-proclaimed superiority over other Brahminical counterparts. When Babujee continued to nurture the illusion of being a kingmaker despite the presence of a '*Kanyakubja*', the latter reciprocated by stopping govt. advertisements to *Nai Duniya*. Perhaps it was a maiden challenge to Babujee's authority. Govt. advertisements constituted the backbone of *Nai Duniya*'s economy as its circulation had not reached the break-even point. Moreover, the paper was also indebted to the financial institutions which had financed the imported machinery. Babujee had no option but to yield to the *Kanyakubja* supremo. While Babujee's supporters still maintain that he never yielded, they find it difficult to explain as to what caused the restoration of advertisements to *Nai Duniya* and who had bowed low to Pandit Mishra at Pachmarhi?

By this time Babujee had realized that his position as a Kingmaker was no more invulnerable. D.P. Mishra, on his part had also learnt that the prevailing situations had demanded a revised strategy. It was this convoluted strategy of pandit D.P.Mishra that diminished the authority of Babujee as a 'journacrat' of formidable repute. But poetic justice awaited Panditjee. His govt. was toppled by the Rajmata of Gwalior when Shri G.N. Singh succeeded him as the fifth Chief Minister of Madhya Pradesh. Panditjee had to wait for quite a long period till his favourite disciple Arjun Singh succeeded the throne after a galaxy of incumbents including Shri K.C.Joshi, Shri V.K.Saklecha, Shri Shyama Charan

Shukla, and Shri P.C. Sethi had already played their innings. With the only exception of Shri Shyama Charan Shukla, all belonged to the old Madhya Bharat region and were totally dependent upon babujee for their 'image', public rating and the political milage. Although Shri S.C.Shukla belonged to Raipur, he was a son-in-law of Indore and had done all those things to the Indorians which were otherwise due to his wife. He was shot into the limelight as a specialist of fast-tract irrigation schemes and had earned the title of 'Ir- rigation King'. For reasons known to Babujee and the then political correspondent of his pulpdom, the said title was never elaborated in the columns of *Nai Duniya*. Alas! The ghost of the D.P.Mishra regime was still haunting the premises of Meeta Nursery. Both Mr. S.C.Shukla and Mr. Ar- jun Singh had started their political career as Ministers in the cabinet of Pandit D.P.Mishra in 1964. Both had wit- nessed Panditji's strategy *vis-à-vis* the pulpdom of Indore. But Mr. Arjun Singh was more committed to the *Kanyakub- ja* stalwart than Mr. S.C. Shukla whose father (the late Pt.Ravi Shankar Shukla) had groomed Pandit D.P.Mishra as the then Home Minister of the old Madhya Pradesh. While Pandit D.P.Mishra expected the Shukla brothers to be docile to him, they continued to treat the old man as their father's "deputy". This offended Panditjee's ego which in turn facilitated the advent of Mr. Arjun Singh, the master blaster of pulp whores. The quintessence of what the Brahmin of Kautilya's repute had transmitted to the Thakur of Churhat was as follows:

I. Since Indore controls the financial strings of Madhya Pradesh politics, a non-Indorian can not thrive as a Chief Minister without controlling the sorceress who in turn, controlled the ghost of finance.

II. The above objective could be achieved through a three-pronged strategy as laid down in the *Panchtantra...*

    (i) If the opponent is weak and vulnerable, throw a piece of bread or cake at him.

    (ii) If you have compatible strength, flight him out.

    (iii)If he is stronger, flatter the fool.

When Mr. Arjun Singh took over as the Chief Minister of Madhya Pradesh, he made it a point not only to implement the *Panchtantra* strategy in its totality but also to demonstrate a repeated gang-rape of the sorceress of pulpdom. To begin with, he instructed the Indore Development Authority to allot prime land at the rate of Rs.3/- per square foot to all those who were either publishing a journal from Indore or had obtained a declaration title for the same from Indore irrespective of their native place. This prime land was situated at the Agra-Bombay Road where leading transport companies were willing to pay Rs.100/- to Rs.300/- per sq.ft. depending upon the situation of the plot. The land was undeveloped and the development cost itself was estimated to be Rs.5/- per sq.ft. or so. When bureaucrats explained this to the CM, he overruled them by maintaining that press owners would be developing the same at their cost. All said and done, the land was allotted at a notional price of Rs.3/- per sq.ft. and an annual lease rent of this or that amount depending upon the size of the plot. Subsequently, the press barons managed to get the land developed at the cost of the govt. Even tabloids and weeklies were obliged. Nai Duniya was not a party to this pulp-conglomerate as it already had its own prime land at Kesar Bagh Road. Covertly, the new press complex at Agra-Bombay Road constituted Mr. Arjun Singh's (read Mahakaushal's) coalition forces against the ex-kingmaker of the rogue State.

The Thakur had already thrown bread crumbs to all those who had a cherished desire to compete with Babujee. There was no need to flatter the fool as the proverbial fool had ceased to be invulnerable. The only remaining principle of Panchtantra that could be applied in the situation was to warrant a clear signal that the king had compatible strength to combat the 'kingmaker'. Hence there was no scope for any power-broker. Thus, Mr. Arjun Singh emerged as the first Chief Minister of Madhya Pradesh who had dragged the disillusioned Kingmaker to the arena on an equal footing. Before him, his mentor had also done so but on a "higher footing", without giving any benefit of doubt to anybody to be equal to the *Kanyakubja* stalwart.

Mr. Arjun Singh had not only tamed the hostile monopolist but had also planted his own 'moles' in almost every newspaper of Indore, Bhopal and New Delhi giving rise to the prolonged debate whether press and the Govt. should be friends or adversaries. In this connection, it will be interesting to note what Mr. Bill D. Moyers, an American journalist and former press Secretary to the U.S. President has observed, "the press and the government are not allies. They are adversaries... Each has a special place in our scheme of things. The president was created by the constitution and the press is protected by the constitution...the one with the mandate to conduct the affairs of the State, the other with the privileges of trying to find out all it can about what is going on. How each performs is crucial to the working of a system that is both free and open but fallible and fragile. For it is the nature of a democracy to thrive upon conflict between press and government without being consumed by it".

The position of the Fourth Estate in India vis-à-vis the three is not different from that prevailing in the U.S., but I do not think the President of USA has ever offered government land to any influential newspaper or had ever connived in the financial manipulations of press barons who were in a position to exploit or blackmail the government of their time. This is a peculiar development in the Indian democracy where the Executive is helpless to take any punitive action against criminals because of their nexus with the press and the politician. Since politicians cannot afford to win any election without the support of the press and criminals, any action against both or either would ultimately reduce the numerical strength of their vote banks. Fluctuating between self- congratulatory Narcissism and a projected Leftist gender, the Indian Press appears to be programmed to improve upon its whoroscope by evolving criminals into demi-gods!

All said and done, Nai Dunia enjoyed *numero uno* position till mid 1990's in the city of Indore. It lost ground to Bhaskar due mainly to its own price tag. By the end of 2007, it regained the numerical strength when it reduced the price from Rs 2.50/ per copy to the amount comparable with the rivals' price tag. Presently, it has 06 editions and has ambitious projects to penetrate into U.P and Rajasthan.

7 The Meteoric Rise Of Bhaskar

When the late Dwarka Prasad Agrawal reached Bhopal in 1956, he had no idea that his family would emerge as leader in the realm of Hindi Journalism. Similarly, when his son, Mr. Ramesh Agrawal performed a *Shatchandi Yajna* along with Mr. Hari Agrawal at Indore, he had little apprehension that the wheat seeds to be germinated for the purpose of *yajna* would yield white blades of grass instead of green ones. This was a miraculous omen as it indicated over-all prosperity of the seeker performing the *yajna*. If my departed friend, Mr. R.N. Agrawal is to be believed, Mr. Ramesh Agrawal has preserved those white blades of grass after getting them duly cleansed and charged with mantras. This sounds more like an episode from "Santoshi Mata ki Katha" but the *dramatis personae* may like to reveal what separates myth from the prevailing reality.

When the Indore edition of Dainik Bhaskar was launched in 1983, it belonged to "they also ran" category as the undivided *Nai Duniya* was the leading light in Hindi journalism, though cash starved and less hypocritically humble than its present avtar. At that time, the present aboriginal editor of *Nai Duniya* had no idea that Bhaskar would outsmart the strategic variety of journalism that he had inherited from his father. Equally unaware was his cognizance that eventually, he would be constrained to hire someone from Dainik Bhaskar's managerial hierarchy to guide him and his team to improve the quality of his product *vis-a-vis* market forces. This happened in November 2005 when Nai Duniya hired Mr. Anil Dhoopar, the then Vice President, Bhaskar group of Publication, to work as Man Friday for Nai Duniya. Perhaps Mr. Chhajlani's ancestors in heaven would never forgive him for such a non-marwari gesture that too, at an astronomical amount of salary hitherto denied to any editor worth his salt (aboriginal editor excluded).

A Brief History of Bhaskar Group

The prototype of Bhaskar was a tabloid called "Dainik Prakash" published from a dilapidated structure at Janhageerabad (Bhopal) while Mr. D.P.Agrawal was living in the Band Master Chauraha locality of old Bhopal. Eventually, it became a broadsheet of 4 pages (costing 07 paise) and assumed the title "Dainik Bhaskar" in March 1958. Mr. Avinash Chandra Roy was its first editor followed by Thakur Shiv Pratap Singh, Shri Syam Sunder Byohar and Govardhan Das Mehta. However, the journal made its presence felt only after Mr. Mahesh Shrivastava joined the editorial team. The Ujjain edition was launched in 1958 and Thakur S.P.Singh moved there. After sometime, Mr. C.L.Parasher also joined him as manager. But the Ujjain edition could not prolong. In terms of technology, what Nai Duniya had achieved in 1966, was achieved by Baskar in 1981 when it installed an off-set machine at Jhansi. It was more than a breakthrough for Mr. Ramesh Agrawal as the machinery at Jhasi helped him to run the show at Gwalior when he was confronting a family feud in 1991. His two step sisters viz., Ku. Hemlata and Ku. Anuradha had claimed ownership of the Gwalior edition founded by their father, Mr. D.P.Agrawal, who was alive. Since Mr. D.P. Agrawal was suffering from parlysis, Ms. Hemlata Agrawal claimed to represent him.

When Mr. Arjun singh assumed charge as the C.M. of M.P. in 1988, he was presumably annoyed with this journal as it had supported the cause of his rivals like Mr. Motilal Vora and the late Madhav Rao Sindhia within the Party. Grapevine has it that under the pretext of "Public unrest" Mr. Arjun Singh prompted the administrative machinery to teach him a lesson. As a result, the police ousted all the employees from the premises of Bhaskar Office at Gwalior and locked the building after midnight. Although, Mr. Arjun Singh maintains that it was a decision taken by the local administration of Gwalior, Mr. Ramesh Agrawal always found it diffuclt to believe him. The entire property of the Gwalior edition was seized. The journal could not be published for a pretty long period. It was during this time that Mr. Ramesh Agrawal kept the show running in make-shift tents and open space where the editorial and managerial staff reported to the boss. As regards printing, this was accomplished at Jhansi, 120 KMs away from Gwalior. Subsequently, the premises and belongings were restored to him after Court's intervention.

Eventually, the Bhaskar Group emerged as the fastest growing chain in the print media with 18 editions of the Hindi daily, Dainik Bhaskar from eight different states, four editions of the Gujrati daily, Divya Bhaskar from Gujrat, an international edition of the same from New York and one edition of Saurashtra Samachar from Bhavnagar. Besides, it also launched an English daily, "DNA" from Bombay in collaboration with Mr. Subhash Chandra Goel of Zee T V fame.

The financial supplement of DNA, "DNA Money" was also launched as an independent financial daily from Indore in January 2006 at a modest price of Re.1/- per copy. Given below is a table that depicts details of all the journals published by the Bhaskar Group except the international edition of its Gujarati journal from New York.

Madhya Pradesh, Chhattisgarh & Maharashtra	
Bhopal (1958)	Jabalpur (1986)
Bilaspur	Mumbai (DNA, 2005)
Gwalior (1967)	Nagpur (2002)
Indore (Dainik Bhaskar 1983)	Raipur (1983)
Indore (DNA MONEY, 2006)	Satna (1983)
Rajasthan	
Ajmer	Kota (1997)
Bikaner	Shri Ganganagar (1998)
Jaipur (1996)	Udaipur (1998)
Jodhpur (1997)	
Punjab, Haryana, HP & UP	
Amritsar (2006)	Jalandhar (2006)
Chandigarh (2000)	Jhansi (1981)
Faridabad (2001)	Panipat (2000)
Hisar (2000)	
Gujarat	
Ahmedabad- Divya Bhaskar (2003)	Rajkot- Divya Bhaskar (2004)
Baroda- Divya Bhaskar (2004)	Surat-Divya Bhaskar (2004)

While nobody would be interested in the chronological details of various editions, financial analysts would be certainly interested in two things: first, whether the Bhaskar Group is a single corporate entity or a convenient alliance of eponymous entities? Second, what is the secret of its financial management? As regards the first question, the nomenclature itself was not a single corporate entity but a package term for the following constituents as recorded in the 1999-2000 yearbook, published by the Indian Newspaper Society:

I.   M/s Writers and Publishers Pvt. Ltd.
II. Bhaskar Graphic and Printing Arts.
III. Bhaskar Publications and Allied Industries Pvt. Ltd.
IV. Bhaskar Prakashan Pvt. Ltd.

When the Supreme Court of India restored the ownership of Dainik Bhaskar to M/s Dwarka Prasad Agrawal and Brothers in July, 2003, the management of the Group headed by Mr. Ramesh Chandra Agrawal issued a clarification by way of advertisement in prominent English and Hindi dailies including those published by the group itself. The aforesaid clarification is being reproduced here without any grammatical comment or correction:

PUBLIC NOTICE

"The Honorable Supreme Court in its decision related to the case of Dainik Bhaskar Group (CA No.4782/96, CA No. 4783/96 and WP No.527/93 has passed an order on 7/7/2003 to maintain the same status which was prevalent on the date prior to June 29, 1992. The management of Dainik

Bhaskar has clarified that as per the records, five editions of Dainik Bhaskar were being published before 29/6/92. Accordingly, five different companies/persons were owning and publishing different editions of Dainik Bhaskar viz., Writers and Publishers Limited from Bhopal, Bhaskar Graphics and Printing Arts Private Limited from Indore, Bhaskar Publication and Allied Industries from Gwalior, Mr. Vishambar Dayal Agrawal, Bhaskar Publication Private Limited from Jabalpur and Mr. Sanjay Agrawal from Jhansi.

M/s Dwarka Prasad Agrawal were not owning or publishing any edition of Dainik Bhaskar from anywhere in the country immediately to the passing of the H.C. order dated 29.6.92.

All the above companies were being run by family members of Mr. Ramesh Agrawal, the late Mr. Vishambhar Dayal Agrawal and Mr. Mahesh Prasad Agrawal. At present also only above companies/persons are publishing different editions of Dainik Bhaskar from various places.

The other parties have misinterpreted the Supreme Court's decision.

The abstract of the decision is as under,

"THE CONSEQUENCE OF THIS ORDER WOULD BE THAT THE PARTIES SHALL BE RELEGATED TO THE SAME POSITION IN WHICH THEY WERE IMMEDIATELY PRIOR TO THE PASSING OF THE ORDER DATED 29/6/92.

The Supreme Court in its order has not said that firm M/s Dwarka Prasad Agrawal and Brothers (regd.) would be the owner of the title of Dainik Bhaskar. Further more this is to inform all concern that Mrs. Hemlata Agrawal had forged the documents of the said partnership firm.

The Deputy Registrar Firms, Society and Chits, Meerut, Uttar Pradesh vide its order No.1227 dated 19/7/2003 has noticed the forgery committed by Mrs.Hemlata Agrawal and have ordered to stay the changed documents. Hence this order restrains Mrs.Hemlata Agrawal, Mrs.Kishori Devi and Mr. Anil Kaushik to act on behalf of the M/s Dwarka Prasad Agrawal and Brothers.

All concerned or esteemed readers, business associates and advertising agencies are hereby informed not to get misled and confused by the rumors, misinterpretation and false informations being spread by the other party.

The legal position has been clearly explained as above and all concerned are requested to act as per the prevalent legal position. For further clarity may visit the website of Supreme Court and see the details of the order of the Honorable Supreme Court. For any further clarification please do mail to us at *legalcell@mp.bhaskarnet.com*.

Dainik Bhaskar Group and its associates reserve their right to initiate appropriate legal proceedings against the other parties for spreading false and baseless rumour about the Group."

While it was never made public as to what transpired between the litigants, entries in the INS yearbook revealed that with the exception of the Jabalpur edition, Mr. Ramesh Agrawal was in full command of all the remaining editions. The Jabalpur edition is owned by Bhaskar Prakashan Ltd. whose Managing Editor, Mr. Kailash Agrawal represents the same in INS. As regards the Gwalior edition, the name of Mr. Devendra Kumar Tiwari appears as the INS representative followed by a clarification "for other details please see Dainik Bhaskar page." "In the latest Handbook published by the INS (2006-2007) there is an additional clarification about the Jabalpur edition that states, "publishers, Bhaskar Prakashan Pvt. Ltd. through Manmohan Agrawal- under contract with Writers & Publishers Ltd...". Presently, 22 editions have been mentioned in the 2007 edition of the INS Handbook under the entry, 'Dainik Bhaskar, Bhopal. As regards Jabalpur edition, it is simultaneously published from Jabalpur, Satna and Nagpur.

A skeptical review of the table on page 3 will reveal that till 1995, the group was confined to M.P. only. During the span of last 10 years, it penetrated Punjab, Haryana, Himachal Pradesh, Rajasthan, U.P., Gujrat, Maharashtra, the Union Territory of Chandigarh and the Big Apple called New York. What could be the key to such a phenomenal success? According to Mr. S.K.Basu, the Manager in-charge, Training and Corporate Communication at he Bhopal Office of Bhaskar, the success is due to innovative management techniques, state of the art technology, professional management and right marketing strategies. I am skeptical about this explanation as it sounds more like an extract from an IIM handout, strategically silent about financial sources. But I don't blame Mr. Basu. Had he known the secret, he would have launched his own chain of newspapers. While the secret is known only to Mr. Ramesh Agrawal and his family members, their own *muneems* and statutory auditors may also be having a vague idea as to what separates "invisibles" from tangible assets. If common friends and prospective partners are to be believed, the strategy is very simple. If you are already a partner or close friend or client or business associate of Mr. Ramesh Agrawal, and if he is planning a new edition say from a city called Mayapur, he may casually ask you *"Mayapur ke liye teri kitnee pantee rakhun?"* "How much share should I assign you for Mayapur edition?" "If you say, 20 Paise", then you may have to shell out Rs.20 Lakh for the Mayapur Project which is estimated to cost Rs. One crore. Profit sharing will also be proportinate but would be restricted only to earnings of Mayapur edition subject of course to the margin on advertisement, procured on the strength of corporate image and given to Mayapur edition "that also ran".

Mr. Murdoch! Have you heard of Agrawals?

Do you mean the guys who first flirt with the STAR and then rape the moon? OKAAY! OKAAY!

8 The Advent Of Journacracy

One Mr. Manoj Yadav, resident of 25 Keshar Bagh Chauki, Babu L.C. Chhajlani Marg, Indore had filed a complaint to the Governor of M.P. on 31.12.2000 inviting His Excellency's attention on the following points *inter alia*:

I. That, he had lodged a complaint to the Ombudsman of M.P. on 18.1.97 against the Chief Minister for the alleged atrocities which resulted in the loss of crores of Rupees to the state Government. The most significant item being the allotment of a plot of land to *Nai Dunia*, (a daily published from Indore) for Rs.5 lakh while the market price of the plot in question was Rs.5 crore or so. The next significant allegation was that the Chief Minister had caused the transfer of land measuring 37,500 square foot belonging to the M.P.Tourism Development Corporation to the Basketball Area Corporation Trust that again resulted in the form of a financial loss to the state Government to the tune of Rs.5 crore.

II. The complainant also alleged that the Ombudsman did not take any action on the said complaint dated 18.1.1997.

III. This was followed by another complaint filed by Mr. Prakashchand Jain of Indore before the First Additional

Sessions Judge on 25.9.1998 under section 13 of the Prevention of Corruption Act and Section 120-B of the IPC against Mr. Digvijay Singh and his 'Param Mitra' (as stated in the complaint), Shri Abhaya Chhajlani, the proprietor of Nai Dunia. As soon as the Ombudsman learnt this, he got Mr. Majoj Yadav's complaint dated 18.1.97 registered on 26.9.98 (after 20 long months) and ordered the submission of an application to the effect that since the matter was already being investigated by the Ombudsman, the suit may be closed at the court concerned.

IV. The complainant maintained that the prolonged delay of twenty long months on part of the Ombudsman was not only against the provisions of Section 12-A of M.P. Lokayukta and Uplokayukta Act 1981, but was also an act that prohibited legal action initiated by him. As if this were not enough, the Ombudsman also managed to get his conclusions published in different newspapers without actually investigating all the allegations. All said and done, the Ombudsman gave a clean chit to the C.M. by stating that his (C.M's) predecessors had also allotted plots of land at concessional rates to the newspapers in conformity with the state Government's policy, dated 10.8.1995. Objecting to this, the complainant maintained that the said policy did not allow any blanket permission to the Chief Minister or his cabinet to reduce the rates at their discretion. However, the implied power was delegated to a committee as laid down in para (2) of the aforesaid Policy. Hence, the Govt's order dated 17.8.95 to allot the said plot of land to Nai Dunia at a concessional price of Rs.5 lakh was an act of corruption under Section 13(1) (D) of the Prevention of Corruption Act. Moreover, as per para (5) of the Govt. of M.P.'s Policy dated 10.8.95, the maximum entitlement of Nai Dunia for such an allotment was restricted to 10,000 sq.ft. as its circulation was below one lakh as on that date. As against that, the land allotted to Nai Dunia admeasured four times more than the prescribed limit. Hence, an act of corruption.

V. The complainant further maintained that Mr. Abhaya Chhajlani had been taking undue advantage of his friendship with Mr. Digbvijay Singh due mainly to the influence of his newspaper. The details of such undue advantages were enumerated as follows:-

    (i) Mr. Abhaya Chhajlani was conferred the status of a minister of state by elevating him to the position of Vice-President of the M.P. Sports Council.

    (ii) The Sports Complex built by the M.P.Table Tennis Trust with the help of public money was allowed to be christened as 'Abhaya - Prashal' by the Chief Minister.

    (iii)Mr. Abhaya Chhajlani failed to submit the accounts relating to the M.P. Table Tennis Lotteries and deposited only Rs.35,98,703/- in the Trust while the figure of exempted tax itself amounted to Rs.12 crore. This necessitated a case of fraud and criminal breach of trust against Mr. Chhajlani. As against this, in a reply addressed to the Hon'ble High Court regarding the contempt of court petition, it was submitted that a charge sheet was filed in the court of the First Judicial Magistrate that leveled a simple charge of non-submission of accounts in respect of the said lotteries. This was a clear case of political protection to Mr. Chhajlani against cognizable offences. In the same para, it was also alleged that admission cards worth more than Rs. one crore were sold, with a view to mobilizing funds for the Khel Prashal (subsequently named as Abhaya Prashal') under the auspices of a musical evening in the name of Lata Mangeshkar who graced the occasion. According to the complainant, Mr. Chhajlani failed to submit accounts pertaining to this event also and deposited only Rs.7,29,891.73 in the Table Tennis Trust. The submission of accounts is obligatory under Section 7 & 8 of the M.P. Entertainment Tax and Advertisement Charges Act in order to qualify for the exemptions thereunder.

VI. Mr. Abhaya Chhajlani also used the premises of Khel Prashal such as the surrounding open space, shops and offices for the purpose of allotment to his friends, relatives and family members on nominal rent. This was done without obtaining prior permission for the purpose as required under Section 14 of the M.P. Public Trusts Act. As such, this act also warranted a criminal case against Mr. Chhajlani under Section 14 of the said Act. As an alternative, Mr. Digvijay Singh could also initiate action to remove the allegedly "criminal trustee" under Section 26 of the M.P. Public Trusts Act. Mr. Digvijay Singh not only failed to take any action under the relevant provisions of the aforesaid Act, but was also instrumental in waiving certain conditions in favour of Mr. Chhajlani for which a special order was issued by the Revenue Deptt. of the Govt. of M.P. vide their letter No.F-6-172/76 dated 26.12.97 signed by the Deputy Secretary, Mr. P.D. Agrawal.

VII.Mr. Digvijay Singh was also instrumental in the creation of "M.P.Nehru Kendra Lalbagh Nyas" which happens to be an illegal creation ab-initio as he had no jurisdiction over the premises that had acquired the status of an archeological heritage. As per the Govt. of M.P.'s order dated 11 September 1998, issued by the Department of Culture, the Board of Trustees of the said Trust consisted of the following:

1. Shri Abhaya Chhajlani, Chairman
2. Shri M.A. Farukhi, Vice-Chairman Principal, Islamia Kasimia, Indore.
3. Shri M.C.Joshi, Trustee, Ex-Director General, Archaeological Survey of India
4. Shri Ashok Chitle, Trustee
5. Dr. Majushri Bhadari, Trustee
6. The Principal Secretary/Secretary Govt. Trustee-Deptt. of Culture.
7. The Principal Secretary/Secretary, Govt. Trustee, Finance Deptt.
8. The Commissioner, Govt. Trustee Indore Division
9. The Commissioner/Director Govt. Trustee, Archaeological Records and Secretary Museums
10. Collector, Indore, Govt. Trustee

As per the notification published in the gazette, objections regarding the proposed trust were invited within 30 days but the trust in question was registered on the 11th day itself and Mr. Chhajlani was given the charge.

While the above cases continued to be sub-judice till these lines were written, it would be interesting to consider whether the evolution of Nai Dunia brand of journalism into "journacracy" was a natural outcome of its re-structured ownership or the re-structuring itself was aimed at journacracy?

The Owners & Successors

As stated earlier, Babujee owned 60% shares of *Nai Dunia* while Mr. Narendra Tiwari and Bhaiyaji alias Mr. B.L.Sethia owned 20% each. Subsequently, the ownership pattern was re-structured within the financial limits of each family as follows:

1	Shri L.C. Chhajlani	
2	Shri Shrichand Chhajlani	Within the 60% shares of Chhajlani family
3	Shri Ajaychand Chhajlani	
4	Shri Vinaychand Chhajlani	
5	Shri Narendra Tiwari	
6	Smt. Mamta Tiwari	Within the 20% shares of Tiwari family
7	Smt. Vimla Tiwari	
8	Shri Basantilal Sethia	
9	Shri Mahendra Kumar Sethia	Within the 20% shares of Sethia family
10	Shri Prem Kumar Sethia	

Whether the re-structuring was aimed at tax-planning or had an ulterior motive was known only to Babujee who re-shuffled his mortal coil on 19th of January 1981. After Babujee's death, the ownership pattern was re-structured as follows:

1. Smt. Gangabai Chhajlani
2. Shri Abhaychand Chhajlani
3. Shri Ajaychand Chhajlani

4. Shri Vinay Chhajlani
5. Shri Shrichand Chhajlani
6. Shri Rahul Barpute
7. Shri Narendra Tiwari
8. Smt. Vimla Tiwari
9. Shri Rajendra Tiwari
10. Shri B.L.Sethia
11. Shri Mahendra K.Sethia
12. Shri Prem K.Sethia

The above arrangement continued till 1985 but was sub-sequently re-structured due to Mr. Narendra Tiwari's demise in the same year. The new structure emerged as follows:

1. Shri B.L.Sethia
2. Shri Mahendra K.Sethia
3. Shri Prem K.Sethia
4. Smt. Gangabai Chhajlani
5. Shri Abhay Chhajlani
6. Shri Shrichand Chhajlani
7. Shri Ajaychand Chhajlani
8. Shri Vinay Chhajlani
9. Shri Rahul Barpute
10. Shri Rajendra Tiwari
11. Smt. Vimla Tiwari
12. Shri Vishwas Tiwari
13. Shri Apoorva Tiwari

It was perhaps in 1988 that the Bhopal edition of *Nai Dunia* was launched which culminated in the split between Tiwari and Chhajlani families in 1991. While the ownership of Bhopal edition remained with Tiwari family, Chhajlanis and Sethias continued to hold the original Indore edition.

However, Mr. Rajendra Tiwari's name continued to appear in the Indore edition dated 1st of March every year from 1992 to 1995. This could be due mainly to the final settlement of accounts which must have been finalized in four to five instalments during 1992 to 1995. Needles to say, the first complaint against the allotment of a plot of land to *Nai Dunia* by the Digvijay Singh govt. became public only in 1997 when Mr. Manoj Yadav reported the same to the Ombudsman of M.P. on 18.1.97. This however does not mean that journacracy was not active before the split of partnership. The split simply facilitated more freedom and autonomy to the parting journacrats as is clear from the following account.

I. The Bhopal Development Authority allotted land to *Nai Dunia* for its Bhopal edition on 16.6.1982. However, this land was inherited by the Tiwari family after partition. Subsequently, "Nai Dunia Printery", a sister concern of the original Nai Dunia, was allotted 40 thousand square metres of land by the M.P.Audyogik Kendra Vikas Nigam at its Rangwasa Industrial Area on 5.9.1997. This was the same piece of land for which an organization of the rural youth had requested allotment with a view to creating job potential in the area.

II. As per the agreement of partition dated 31.3.1991, it was agreed between both the parties that the Bhopal edition called *Dainik Nai Dunia* would not be sold in the Indore & Ujjain Divisions while the original Nai Dunia published from Indore would not be sold in the Bhopal Division as also in an adjoining one. But destiny appeared to bless Mr. Chhajlani on this count also. One, Mrs. Shakeela Begum had been publishing a weekly entitled *Rajya Ki Nai Dunia* from Bhopal. Mr. Chhajlani managed to purchase this tabloid in the name of his

Bhopal Bureau Chief, Mr. Umesh Trivedi. After the change of ownership, this tabloid also created history being the first weekly in Bhopal to have received govt. advertisement worth Rs. one lakh on a single count. Subsequently, Mr. Umesh Trivedi transferred the ownership rights of this weekly to his employer's company entitled M/s Nai Dunia communication Pvt.Ltd. on 05.06.1996. The same weekly has since been converted into a daily awaiting separate allocation of land from the "govt. that be" as the original plot meant for the Bhopal edition (re-christened as *Dainik Nai Dunia*) now rests with the Tiwari family.

III. There are more than 70 public charity trusts of the Jain community registered at Indore, the most significant being those which control the prime commercial premises in the Sarafa locality of Indore. Needless to say, not a single trust of the community in question can afford to function independently without acknowledging the governing influence of the Chhajlani family or its patronage. Besides, the family itself has floated the following trusts:

    (i) Babu Labhchand Chhajlani Trust,
       (Registration No.130/81-82)
    (ii) Nai Dunia Jan Seva Trust
       (Registration No.567-31/3/97)
    (iii)Chhajlani foundation
       (Registration No.604-17/7/98)

As if this were not enough, green leaves have refused to unflutter without Mr. Chhajlani's permission in the premises of the following trusts:

    I. Table Tennis Trust, 88 Vasudewva nagar Indore.
    II. Corporation Area Basketball Trust Indore.

III.   (Registration No.131/81-82)

IV. Shri Ramchandra Neema Smriti SRP. Trust Indore (Registration No. 118)

V. M.P. Cricket Association Trust (Registration No.118)

VI. M.P. Mahila Cricket Trust. (Registration No. 252/20.8.86)

VII.M.P.Nehru Kendra Lal Bagh Trust, Lal Bagh Palace Indore. (Registration No.616-11-9-98)

VIII.Princess Sharda Raje Holker Charitable Trust, 48 Annapurna Road, Indore.

IX. Shri Prakash Chand Sethi Charitable Trust & Research Foundation B-14 Ratlam Kothi Indore (Registration No.527/29.1.96).

X. The School of Plastic Surgery, Ganga Jamuna Apartment, South Tukoganj, Indore (Registration No. 510/28.1.95).

XI. Abhinava Kala Samaj etc. Trust, Indore (Registration No.327/30.1.89).

XII.Sethia Foundation, 646 Vijay Nagar, Dashehra Maidan Road Indore (Registration No.316/31.10.88).

XIII.Her Highness Maharani Sahiba Indira Bai Holker Trust, 29 Manik Bagh Road, Indore (Registration No. 247/15.5.86).

XIV.Shri Mishrilal Gangwal Public Charity Trust A-25 MIG Colony Indore (Registration No.199/6.9.84).

XV.Devi Ahilyabai Holker Education Trust Manik Bagh Indore (Registration No.96/18.8.80).

Meanwhile, *Nai Dunia* continues to write pontifical editorials against corruption and negotiating with all those who feel offended by what has been written or hinted about them in the esteemed journal of *Shab-e-Malwa*.

Holier Than Thou

The story of *Nai Duniya* may prompt us to believe that other major dailies published from the Mecca of Hindi journalism are perhaps free from any stigma! Unfortunately the stigma is more fortunate than its negation. According to newspaper reports published in significant dailies of M.P. (on October 27, 2004) the Bhopal Cleaning House was practically paralyzed on October 26, 2004 due mainly to the astronomical no. of bounced cheques issued by a plantation company. This plantation company was none other than the Enbee Plantation Company owned by the Maheshwari family that publishes the multi edition Hindi daily, *Nava Bharat* from M.P., Chatteesgarh and Maharashtra as also the English daily, *Central Chronicle*.

The Bhopal based Enbee Plantations Ltd. had floated a lucrative scheme in 1996 that enabled it to collect a whooping amount of Rs.122 crore from more than 1.75 lakh investors, promising them multiplied returns on their investment. Alas! the moon that was promised, proved to be a chimera. Felt cheated by the company, the investors formed Enbee Depositors' Welfare Association, (EDWA) which moved the Nagpur Bench of the Bombay High Court seeking arrest of the company's directors as also attachment of their properties. The directors of the company, among others, also included a Congress Rajya Sabha member, P.K.Maheshwari (should we include the prefix, Mr. or the suffix, 'jee'?). Earlier on the directions of the Nagpur Bench, police investigation teams were sent to Bhopal, Pune and Aurangabad in search of the company directors and their properties.

The Bhopal Municipal Corporation (BMC) was also requested by the police team to give details of the property owned by the aforesaid directors so that the same could be attached. However, reducing democracy to a programmed farce, the BMC failed to oblige the police team that had arrived from Maharashtra. Majority of depositors who had moved the court were from Maharashtra because of a statutory provision there that protects depositors' interests in financial institutions. According to EDWA, the High Court Bench's order asking the Nagpur Police Commissioner to arrest all the seven directors of the plantation company was quickly stayed by the M.P. High Court. However, Justice M.P. Mishra of MPHC ordered constitution of a committee to negotiate modalities of payment and compromise between the company and the creditors holding debentures.

The company was allegedly engaged in the business of high density agro-forestry-based activities. During 1996-98 it had invited public investments from willing investors in the country by floating three different schemes and netted over Rs.120 crore. According to newspaper reports, the company had conceded before the Nagpur High Court that it had to pay at least Rs.66 crore to the investors in addition to the payment worth Rs.90 crore in cash or kind. However many investors have complained that the company shrewdly converted their debentures into equity shares of the company resulting in non-payment of their dues. According to the petitioner, Mr. Deepak Babbanrao Girdhar who spoke to the press, the investors had to struggle a lot through several courts to get a meeting convened as the company management had an upper hand in the political hierarchy of those who mattered in the Government. Ultimately, when the meeting was held at Bhopal on November 15, 2003 the company proposed a fresh scheme to goad the investors futher. This annoyed them and the debenture holding creditors did not allow the retired High Court judge to chair the meeting.

The company issued a press release that blamed the group of investors who disrupted the meeting thereby depriving large no. of investors interested in casting their vote by using the ballot paper. In other words, the gullible ones who were willing to be goaded by the fresh scheme, were not allowed to be befooled by those who allegedly disrupted the meeting. Further, the company claimed that it had already distributed money to 70% depositors and was planning to repay the remaining ones in a phased manner.

The defrauded depositors from Punjab, Maharashtra, Chhattisgarh, Delhi and other parts of the country had reached Bhopal under the impression that they would receive their dues. Accordingly, the crowd demanded physical presence of the directors, namely-P.K. Maheshwari, Sandeep Maheshwari and others and shouted slogans against the company and demanded immediate attachment of their properties in Mumbai, Bhopal, Nagpur and other places, failing which they insited for the arrest of the company directors responsible for the fraud. To their surprise, they discovered that none of the Maheshwaris had turned up instead, some 'dummy directors' were representing the company on the spot. Justice Singh, the arbitrator appointed by the Hon'ble High Court agreed that the investors' demands were genuine but added that he had come there only to know their opinion about the acceptability of the proposed fresh scheme and that the final decision would be taken by the High Court. The investors in turn, apprised the arbitrator of their intention to oppose the fresh proposal by raising their hands against it and also refused to fill any form. All said and done, they unanimously opposed Enbee Plantation's new plan that advocated waiver of interest on debentures and payment of principal amount in three equal installments. Calculated at the minimum, the company had to pay a whooping sum of Rs.47.37 crore to the investors as the principal alone besides additional amount payable as interest for over five years.

The furious investors also blamed the Congress Government and alleged that the M.P. Government was hand in glove with the Company and hence the police at Bhopal were taking no action against the Maheshwaries. P.K. Maheshwari is a Rajya Sabha member of the party. Criticizing the State Government for being soft on the Maheshwaris despite thousands of cases registered against them across the State, they maintained that relevant provisions of the 'Protection of Interest of Investors Act 2001' were not being invoked to book them.

The Act Of Economic Offence Wing

According to newspaper reports published in significant English & Hindi dailies with Bhopal dateline (July 24, 2004) the Economic Offence Wing (EOW) had registered a case of fraud against the former ministers, several IAS Officers and 42 companies in connection with the Rs.719 crore scam involving non-repayment of loans granted by Madhya Pradesh State Industrial Corporation (MPSIDC) under the Inter-Corporate-Deposit Scheme (ICD). MPSIDC had disbursed short term loans of Rs. 639 crore to several companies since 1995, but a big chunk of loans were not repaid. The loans were granted for a period ranging from three to six months and the due amount with interest had risen to Rs.719 crore.

After investigation into the alleged case of misappropriation, the management of MPSIDC found that the then Management of Corporation was involved in serious economic irregularities. Loans worth crores of Rs. were sanctioned without accepting the project report or applications. Some companies registered with Board for Industrial & Financial Reconstruction (BIER) were also given loans which could surprise the BIFR.

It was found that the entire amount of loans was disbursed without even ascertaining whether the earlier amount had been utilized. Further, despite the loans being short-term, the timing for refunding the loan amount was extended repeatedly. In fact, the State Government had stopped giving term loans in 1993-94, but the then Board of directors including former chairman Rajendra Kumar Singh, Ajay Acharya, J.S. Rammurthi and M.P. Rajan started the new process of granting loans under the ICD Scheme. Further, investigations revealed that the then MDs, M.P. Rajan, S.R. Mohanti & Chairman Narendra Nahta deliberately kept the loans unsecured.

On the basis of MPSIDC's report the State Government finally directed the EOW to register cases of fraud, forgery of valuable security, forgery for the purpose of cheating and criminal breach of trust under Section 409, 420, 467, 468 and 120 (B) of the IPC against former ministers Narendra Nahta and Rajendra Kumar Singh, other MPSIDC Board members like M.P. Rajan, S.R. Mohanti, Ajay Acharya, J.S.Rammurti (all bureaucrats) apart from 42 defaulting companies. The list of defaulting companies published in the Hindustan Times dated 25th July 2004 also included "Enbee Industries" (connected with the Maheshwari family that publishes the Hindi daily, Nava Bharat) and M/s Bhaskar Industries of Mr. Agrawal connected with the Hindi journal, Dainik Bhaskar. While the HT had publisheds the names of all the companies involved, the same news item published in the *Rajya ki Nai Duniya* (RKD) was strategically silent about the names of the companies. Was it due to an apprehension of *quid-pro-quo* or otherwise, is known only to the corporate entities controlling the publication during the period under report. One thing that has crystallized the coverage is that the regional/modem editions of national dailies like Hindustan Times and Times of India are not interested in the inter-personal rivalry of the regional press barons unless it affects either their circulation or the revenue prospects in terms of Government advertisements.

The above news item had no significance for the Delhi edition of the same newspaper that gave it a double column coverage on 25.07.2004 and a five column coverage on 27.07.2004 in the Bhopal edition. At that time, it was difficult to believe that the publication of this story could result in the form of loss of chair to then chief minister of M.P. as is clear from the following observation of MS Uma Bharti revealed to the press on 17th of December 2004 at Bhopal:

"संपादक व पत्रकार ईमानदारी से काम करना चाहें तो भी वे नहीं कर सकते। अख़बार मालिकों के धंधे आड़े आ जाते हैं। अख़बार चलाना व्यवसाय बन गया है...जब मैं मुख्यमंत्री थी तो मुझे पता चला कि एक अख़बार के मालिक ने हज़ारों गरीबों का पैसा हड़प लिया है। करोड़ों रुपये डकार कर स्वयं को दीवालिया घोषित कर दिया। स्वयं डिफाल्टर है और मर्सिडीज में घूम रहा है। मैंने उन्हें नोटिस दिया तो मेरी सरकार के घटिया और ख़राब कह कर बदनाम किया गया।"

Free Translation: The editor and scribes cannot work honestly even if they want to do so. The business affairs of the proprietor obstruct their functioning as the publication of newspaper itself has become a business... When I was the chief minister, I came to know that the owner of a particular newspaper had deprived thousands of poor people of their money. Having devoured crores of Rupees he declared himself an insolvent. Despite being a defaulter he was traveling in a Mercedes. When I issued him a notice he defamed my Government by calling it bad and deplorable.

On July 24, 2004 it was difficult to believe that the Sadhvi, who had to relinquish the job of C.M. temporarily due to court case in Karnataka would be permanently denied her job and that she would be constrained to refer to these notices once again. When the top leaders of her party agreed to consider a new chief minister for M.P. in the last week of November 2005, the party spokesman revealed to the press (on November 27) that Mr. Shivraj Singh Chauhan would be the next Chief Minister. Next day, i.e. on November 28, the Bhopal edition of *Dainik Bhaskar* published the following news item as its first lead:

आत्महत्या करने जा रही हूं सुसाइड नोट भिजवा रही हूं ...अणिमा

" नई दिल्ली 27 नवंबर: म.प्र.का मुख्यमंत्री शिवराजसिंह चौहान को बनाए जाने से नाराज़, व्यथित उमा भारती ने बीती रात सबको चौंका दिया। उन्होंने लगभग आधी रात म.प्र.के प्रभारी महासचिव,अरुण जेटली से फोन पर कहा, मैं आत्महत्या करने जा रही हूं। अपने ड्राइवर के साथ सुसाइड नोट भिजवा रही हूं।

Free Translation:GOING TO COMMIT SUICIDE SENDING SUICIDE NOTE...Agnima. "New Delhi, November 27: Annoyed and depressed with the news of Shivraj Chouhan's appointment as CM of MP, Uma Bharti surprised all, last night. Around midnight she phoned Mr. Arun Jaitley, General Secretary I/C of Madhya Pradesh affairs, "I am going to commit suicide, the driver is reaching with the suicide note."

This emotional drama of Uma Bharti continued till 2.30 a.m.

The Proposal regarding Chauhan's name was to be approved by the state legislature party on November 2005 in the presence of party observers Mr. Arun Jaitley and Mr. Pramod Mahajan. When Mr. Chauhan's name was declared,

Uma Bharti insisted that the election should be through secret ballot and no chief minister should be imposed from New Delhi.

This was not adhered to and she was constrained to walk-out along with her supporters. Clearly, this was a case of violation of the democratic procedure and the Sadhvi was justified on this count. This was followed by a pandemonium outside the BJP Office allegedly by the supporters of MS Bharti resulting in lathi charge by police on the party workers at the instance of those very leaders who were elected by these workers. MS Uma Bharti addressed the media on the spot followed by an urgently convened press conference at her Civil Lines residence where she flashed a copy of *Dainik Bhaskar* and said,

"सरकार के 12 करोड़ रुपये खा कर बैठा यह अख़बार एक वर्ष से मेरे चरित्र-हनन पर उतारू हैं। इसलिए मेरे बारे में मनगढ़ंत ख़बरें छाप रहा है।... दैनिक भास्कर में में मेरी आत्महत्या संबंधी खबर से बेहूदा और घटिया बात हो ही नहीं सकती।यह बहुत कुत्सित, घृणित और निंदनीय कृत्य है...मैंने मुख्यमंत्री काल में इस अख़बार समेत सभी बकायादारों को भी नोटिस दिये थे, तब भास्कर के मालिक, रमेशचंद्र अग्रवाल ने फोन पर मुझसे गिड़गिड़ाते हुए कहा था कि इस नोटिस से उनकी (भास्कर की) इज्ज़त मिट्टी में मिल गई है।तब मैंने उन्हें आश्वस्त किया था कि यदि वे निर्दोष होंगे तो उचित कार्रवाई की जाएगी... यदि अख़बार की नीयत साफ थी तो उन्हें मुझसे भी बात करनी थी, लेकिन ऐसा नहीं करके उन्होंने सिद्ध किया कि अख़बार बदले की भावना से काम कर रहा है।...मेरी कल श्री अरुण जेटली जी से रात 10.30 बजे फोन पर बात हुई थी, तब उनकी पत्नी भी उनके साथ थीं, जबकि दैनिक भास्कर ने साफ झूठ लिखा कि मैंने रात 2.30 बजे श्री जेटली से बात की... सिर्फ़ पैसा कमाने और अख़बार की प्रसार संख्या बढ़ाने के लिए दूसरे की प्रतिमा खंडित करना अनुचित है।"

Free Translation:"(Ms Uma Bharti alleged) that after having devoured Rs.12 crore of the Government this newspaper has resorted to my character assassination for the last one year and has, therefore been publishing fictitious news about me. No news item can be more grotesque, more deplorable, more ridiculous and absolutely baseless than the one regarding my suicide...During my tenure as chief minister, I had issued notices to defaulters including the newspaper concerned. At that time the proprietor, Mr. Rameshchand Agrawal minced words and conveyed to me over telephone that the notice in question had spoilt his (Bhaskar's) reputation. I had assured him then that suitable action would be taken if he was found innocent...

If the newspaper had no malafide intention, they should have consulted me. Having failed to do so, they have confirmed the feeling of vendetta... Last night, I had talked to Mr. Arun Jaitley over telephone at 10.30 p.m., his wife was also there... The paper resorted to sheer falsehood by publishing that I talked to Mr. Jaitley at 2.30 a.m. It is unfair to malign somebody's image with a view to earning money and to increase circulation figures of the newspaper."

When contacted by journalists to explain his position, Mr. Agrawal maintained that he had already re-paid the amount of loan to MPSIDC together with interest and that he would be seeking legal remedy against the Sadhvi by way of defamation suit.

9 The Mutation In Indian Press

The Indian Press, which was by and large a British legacy, hibernated for 30 long years after independence till it woke up with a terrible jerk when the nightmare of the Emergency called it a day. The post-Emergency scenario constrained the judiciary and the Fourth Estate to re-examine the basic framework that had rendered the Constitution vulnerable to the whims of Mrs. Indira Gandhi. As a result, Mr. Nani Palkiwala returned to India after relinquishing his position, as Indian Ambassador in USA with a view to rescuing democracy from the bleeding that ensued the 42nd Amendment of the Indian Constitution.

For a while, it appeared that NRIs were more concerned with the future of democracy than the lesser mortals living in India. The advent of 'India Today', the emergence of 'Indian Express' as the largest chain of a multi- edition English daily, the birth of 'Telegraph' on the horizons of 'The Statesman', the launch of 'Sunday Observer' by Mr. Vinod Mehta in Bombay where Mr. Behram Contractor had already launched two tabloids in quick succession, the birth of *Jansatta* as the Hindi counterpart of the Indian Express had all heralded a new era in the Indian print media. But the most significant mutation manifested itself in the form of the "Indian Post" launched by the Singhanias of "Raymonds" fame. Since coming events cast their shadows before, Mr. Sameer Jain was more than terrified. The Emergency had already jolted him when the Old Lady of Boribunder was molested by a post-andropause receiver appointed by the Government of India. Mr. S. Nihal Singh, was the first star editor of the 'Indian Post' who had a remunerative edge over his counterparts in India. The journal used state of the art technology and computerized processing right from the original draft to the finally approved copy. Downloading was a norm rather than exception and the revised copy could be uploaded as per requirement. Today it sounds familiar but during 1988-89 it was the dawn of a maiden technology that necessitated thick pay packets to every sub-editor who could type on a computer. Those were the days of DOS and Apple Macintosh when the "Window" of Microsoft was hardly visible. There was a mushroom growth of computer training centers in Bombay where semi-literate vendors used to charge a hefty sum of Rs.18,000/- (Repeat Rs.Eighteen Thousand) for teaching DOS commands. This was accomplished with the help of an instructor who was paid a consolidated amount of Rs. 2000/- p.m. as remuneration. Those knowing "Cobol" were considered luminaries in "Computer Science" as the generalized nomenclature, "Information Technology" was still in the embryo. Under the circumstances, Mr. Sameer Jain rightly discerned the writing on the wall and decided to launch an antidote to "The Indian Post" in the form of "The Independent" without disturbing the pages and wages of the Times of India. A new breed of computer savvy journalists (say dignified typists) was recruited in the editorial team led by Mr. Anil Dharkar. And by the way, who was Anil

Dharkar? Well, professionally, he was an academic engineer teaching mechanical engineering at Glasgow where he married a poetess of Pakistani origin. (Since divorced) After returning to India, he first edited 'Debonair' and subsequently, a tabloid called 'Mid Day', founded by Behram Contractor but funded by the family of Khalid Ansari that also owned *Inquilab*. Mr. Sameer Jain had taken a strategic decision that aimed to kill one bird while saving another with the same stone. 'Mid Day' had already carved a niche first in the market share of the 'Evening News of India' (since folded) and then that of the TOI.

For Mr. Dharkar, it was a quantum jump from the narrow lanes of tabloid journalism to the highway fo mainstream broadsheets intending to compete directly with the 'Indian Post' and indirectly with the Washington Post'! Vinod Mehta was another celebrity kicking in the embryo of maiden fame. To begin with, he edited the 'Debonair' and then 'Mid Day' till he launched his own Weekly, "Sunday Observer" in collaboration Mr. Ashwin Shah of 'Jaico' fame. Destiny appeared to be in favour of Mr. Sameer Jain. It was the dawn of globalization and financial reforms but the system was still not free from the Lincence Raj. An editorial comment in the *Indian Post* had offended the government that in turn, adversely affected the business interests of the Singhanias and their corporate identity as "J.K. Group" and "Raymonds". Counselling to the editor resulted in the form of his resignation. This created an opportunity for Mr. Vinod Mehta who was recruited as the new chief editor. Subsequently, Mr. Vijaypat Singhania realized that business activities and journalistic sermons could not proceed hand in hand. He decided to fold the newspaper that intended to revolutionize the print media in India.

Mr. Sameer Jain spared no time to induct Mr. Vinod Mehta as the new chief editor of the "Independent". Although there was no threat from any established press baron, Sameer Jain was aware that Mr. Mehta had the potential to seduce any industrialist for the pulp-whore to whom he was a fashion designer. How prophetic were his observations became perceptible only when Mr. Mehta designed *Shararas* for "Pioneer" and a T-Shirt with inbuilt brassieres for "Outlook."

The unexpected closure of *Indian Post* was a willing suspension of disbelief into belief for Mr. Sameer Jain. He had rescued the TOI from prospective rivals but it was a difficult choice to retain Mr. Mehta on an astronomical amount of salary for grooming an apprentice pulp-whore while seasoned brothel keepers, capable of handling the most unpredictable whore, were available at a monthly salary of Rs. 60,000 plus. The drama would not have reached its climax without an anti-hero. This anti-hero emerged out of the blue, when it was alleged in a news item published in the "Independent" that the late Mr. Y.B. Chavan was a CIA mole. This triggered agitations among the sons of the soil. Accepting moral responsibility, Mr. Vinod Mehta resigned. And the rest is history created by Mr. Mehta and photocopied by the Rahejas.

When Mr. Mehta vacated the editor's chair in the *Sunday Observer*, Rahul Singh, the son of Mr. Khushawant Singh succeeded him as editor. Subsequently, the paper was purchased by Dhirubai Ambani who had locked horns with Mr. Goenka and was restless to launch a daily, that could 'tame' the indomitable Marwari.

This was not possible without a ferocious tiger. The search ended when a Royal Bengal Tiger released by Mr. Sameer Jain was spotted. This 'tiger' was none other than

Mr. Pritish Nandy who himself was destined to be tamed by another tiger of Shiv Sena fame (in due course). Mr. Nandy joined as the chief editor and the paper was renamed, *Economic & Political Observer*. The new office was set-up at Tulsiani Chambers, Nariman Point. As luck would have it, when Mr. Nandy vacated the editor's chair, Mr. Ambani grew 'wiser'. But the latter had already paid a very heavy price for this 'wisdom' in the form of remuneration/honorarium/perks paid to the former. Thus, Mr. Nandy emerged as the mentor of both, the Marwaris and Gujaratis in the realm of financial management within editorial limits.

In hindsight, the majority of press barons realized that they could assume the role of chief editor with the help of sub-editors and the editorial incumbent was unwarranted. However, those conscious of stress-management/mental health factors and their own functional incompetence due to various reasons were constrained to retain the incumbent under the direct supervision of the editorial director. Eventually, one healthy result of this development became perceptible. "No chief editor could negotiate the outcome of a withheld news item without involving the owners except when the owner himself happened to be the chief editor." Here lies the bone of contention. Since Punjabi brand managers are supposed to have an edge over their Marwari and Gujarati counterparts, the NRIs of Punjabi origin first appointed Mohini Bhullar as editorial director when they launched *India Today*. The lady continued to be *numero uno* in the editorial hierarchy of all the periodicals published by the group for more than two decades. It was at her instance that the group had folded the monthly city magazine, *Bombay*. The magazine was devoted to the celebs and events of Bombay. It was this magazine that inspired Mr. Sameer Jain to introduce 'page 3 perverts', a fact that he would find difficult to refute.

The Gist of post-Emergency Reforms

The post-Emergency mutation in the Indian Press can be attributed to the following factors:

I. The emergence of the 'Indian Express' as the first largest chain of multi-edition newspapers which in turn, motivated other press barons to launch regional editions of their respective journals. The trend had a phenomenal repercussion on the language press.

II. The emergence of tabloids in the metropolitan cities as a serious and reliable enterprise although the same is considered to be 'second-grade' in small cities. Tabloids like 'MID DAY' and the 'Afternoon Despatch and Courier' in Bombay continued to be a cause of envy for Mr. Sameer Jain for more than a decade till all the tabloids lost ground due to the emergence of round-the-clock news and views channels.

III. The emergence of glossy news and views weeklies like *India Today* followed by *Outlook* presented a compact account and analysis of major events during the week with due skepticism for the coverage already published in the so-called national dailies. While *India Today* is alleged to be pro-BJP, it is *Outlook* which is at times 'more royal than the king' or should we say queen?

IV. The extension of the 'Indian Post' factor with reference to the city of Bombay and the need to improve upon the quality of journalism elsewhere.

V. The financial sector reforms and the process of globalization of the Indian economy initiated by the Govt. of India in 1990's facilitated foreign investment in media resulting in the mushroom growth of TV channels and the participation of foreign equity in the print media (enter Murdoch!).

The cumulative affect of these reforms transformed the print-media scenario beyond recognition. If the latest handbook (2006-2007) of the Indian Newspaper Society (INS) is any indication, its 673 members are jointly engaged in the publication of 393 dailies, 95 weeklies, 35 fortnightlies, 135 monthlies and 15 other publications of different periodicities. Since new enterprisers are not members, the actual no. of journals and periodicals could be much more than what has been reported in the INS yearbook. The total no. of copies published by the members is 5,10,59463. Language wise, Hindi commands the *numero uno* position followed by English and Marathi. While 207 journals including 153 dailies are published in Hindi, the no. of English journals is 167 that includes 58 dailies. The total no. of Marathi journals is 44 out of which 37 are dailies. Given below is the list of dailies published from more than two places with individual or joint circulation of more than one lakh copies. Incidentally, it is clarified that single edition newspapers irrespective of their circulation have not been included in these figures. Further, it is also clarified that the list is not exhaustive. There may be many more dailies with more than one lakh circulation of which I may not be aware.

Hindi Dailies

Sr.No.	Name of the Journal	Editions
1	Aaj	11

2	Amar Ujala	15
3	Dainik Bhaskar	38
4	Dainik Jagran	31
5	Deshbandhu	5
6	Nai Dunia	5
7	Nav Bharat	9
8	Rajsthan Patrika	20
9	Prabhat Khabar	7
10	Punjab Kesri	10
11	Dainik Tribune	3
12	Purvanchal Prahari	3

English Dailies

Sr.No.	Name of the Journal	Editions
1	Asian Age	4
2	Business Standard	7
3	Deccan Herald	6
4	Deccan Chronicle	7
5	Economic Times	8
6	Financial Express	9 + 1 Gujarati
7	The Hindu	12
8	The Hindu Businessline	14
9	Hindusthan Times	4
10	Hitvada	3

11	Indian Express	10
12	New Indian Express	14
13	Pioneer	6
14	The Statesman	4
15	The Times of India	9
16	The Tribune	4

Other Dailies

Sr.No.	Name of the Journal	Language	Editions
1	Andhra Jyoti	Telugu	20
2	Andhra Prabha	Telugu	7
3	Asomiya Pratidin	Assamese	4
4	Dinamani	Tamil	4
5	Eenadu	Telugu	23
6	Gavkari	Marathi	4
7	Kannada Prabha	Kannada	4
8	Malyala Manorama	Malyalam	12
9	Mathrubhumi	Malyalam	12
10	Maalai Malar	Tamil	8
11	Madhyamam	Malyalam	9
12	Manglam Daily	Malyalam	4
13	Prajashakti	Telugu	8
14	Prajavani	Kannada	7
15	Pudhari	Marathi	9

16	Punjabi Tribune	Punjabi	3
17	Sakal	Marathi	9
18	Sandesh	Gujrati	5
19	Sambad	Oriya	8
20	The Samaj	Oriya	6
21	Thanthi	Tamil	4
22	Samyukta Karnataka	Kannada	5
23	Taruna Bharat	Marathi	3
24	Udayavani	Kannada	3
25	Utkal Mail	Oriya	5
26	Uttar Bang Sambad	Bengali	3
27	Vaarttha	Telugu	19
28	Vijay Karnataka	Kannada	10

10 The Impact of DNA

DNA (the abbreviation of **Daily News and Analysis** without the Definite Article) launched on July 30, 2005 from Bombay continues to be the first newspaper in India that has two Chairmen on its Corporate Board. The launch witnessed an unprecedented deluge in Bombay but the journal was all set to demonstrate corporate exhibitionism on its edit-page. The maiden issue had 54 pages priced at Rs.2/-. What baffled the common man was the photograph of Dawood Ibrahim on the front page captioned, "Do you know this man?"

Perhaps it was not a good omen to begin with the picture of a mafia don on the first day! The maiden editorial on the front page stated among other things, "As Mumbai endures a difficult passage through extra-ordinary days, we launch our city's newest newspaper.... The trust of family members-- of three lakh subscribers ... several times more readers....."

The conventional lay-out of 8 columns was reduced to six columns with wider space. Page no. 2 superscribed as "DNA speak-up" was assigned to readers, page 3 to 8 were filled with city news, the caption of page no. 9 being "Vision 2020", page no. 10 captioned "opinion" appeared to be the edit page. Vital Statistics of corporate exhibitionism were displayed in a box reproduced below:

Ramesh Chandra Agrawal Subhash Chandra Goel
Chairmen

Editor	**Board of Directors**
Gautam Adhikari	Girish Agarwal
Editorial Board	Himanshu Mody
Ayaz Memon	Pawan Agarwal
Arti Jerath	Pradeep Guha
Bipul Guha	Punit Goenka
Khalid Mohammed	Sudhir Agarwal
Malvika Sanghvi	**Publisher**
R. Jagnnathan	M. Venkataraman
Sathya Saran	**Sales & Marketing**
Siddharth Bhatia	Suresh Balkrishnan
Vinay Kamat	**Group Heads**
Section Heads	Abhay Desai
Abhilash Khaitan	A.L.Sriram
Abhijit Majumdar	Amiy Roy
Jamal Sheikh	Gurneesh Khurana
Jit Ray	Jayesh Asher
Manjula Sen	N.B.Verma
Meenakshi Shedde	Parthsarthi Sen
N. Raghuraman	Pramod Dabke
P.S.Leena	Prathap Ravidranath
Priya Tanna	Rajlakshmi Mohan
Raj Nambisan	Rizwan Khatri
Rehan Ansari	Sheena Saji
Sachin Kalbag	
Smita Deshmukh	
Sumit Chokraberty	
Uma Prabhu	

Further, Page No. 11,12 and 13 marked, "India" were devoted to national news from different regions. Page 14 was superscribed "Evolution" while four pages (from page No.13 to 18) were devoted to international news. This was followed by a pink pull-out of eight pages marked DNA MONEY.(From page No.19 to 26); a white pull-out of six pages entitled DNA SPORT (from page No.28 to 32); one more pull-out of 10 pages captioned "After Hours" (Celebs, film stars, Zodiac and dress sense) from page no. 33 to 42); another pull-out of eight coloured pages devoted to real estate matters. At length, there was a glossy supplement of four pages entitled "Life 360o" that depicted different life styles of culture-vultures, shopping, restaurants and travel.

Board of Directors

While both the chairmen do not need any introduction, it is incidentally clarified that Girish, Pawan and Sudheer are Mr. Ramesh Chandra Agarwal's sons. As against this, Mr. Subhash Goel has nominated only one family member as director viz.; Mr. Punit Goenka. The other two directors are highly acclaimed professionals. Mr. Pradeep Guha had led the TOI group for almost three decades before joining Mr. Goel's T.V. channel as its Chairman and Chief Executive. The other nominee, Mr. Himanshu Mody is considered to be a heavyweight in the realm of hijacking telecast rights of cricket matches.

Editorial Board

Mr. Gautam Adhikari, who once appeared to succeed Mr. H.K.Dua (if not Mr. Dileep Padgaonkar) as Chief Editor of the TOI had worked as Executive Editor there. At the DNA Office, the same person created history as the highest paid non-aboriginal editor. The management of DNA in consultation with Mr. Adhikari spared no time to recruit twice-born/ thrice-born siblings of the Old Lady who were rewarded with the accumulated increments of their previous incarnations plus a hefty margin of 50 to 60 percent due mainly to the counter-offers made by Mr. Sameer Jain through his Man Friday. As a result, Mr. Subhash Chandra inadvertently emerged as the numero uno paymaster to the meandering lot of our cash-starved journalists. However, this delayed the break-even-point at the DNA Office. For the conventional muneems of HIndi dailies, the salary bill of the editorial staff of DNA would have sufficed to manage the editorial wages of twenty editions. The only solace for the management was the contractual nature of these appointments and the future of strategic alliances. Visualising rain makers, highly motivated professionals were recruited as Media Planners/Marketing Adhikaris to improve the bottomline of the Corporate Balance Sheet.

The impact on the TOI

Since the dummy copies of the DNA were already available to the chosen few, the Times of India dated July 30, 2005 also had 56 pages, priced at Rs.4/- (inclusive of a complementary copy of Mumbai Mirror worth Rs.2/-). The re-restructuring of contents and layout was also worth noticing. The main paper consisted of 24 pages with four different pull-outs:

I. The first pull-out had 8 pages incorporating the following items:
Page no.25: Times International
Page no.26: Times Classified

Page no.27: Times International

Page no.28: Times Trends

Page no.29: Times International

Page no.30 : Editorial, leader, letters to the editor "speaking tree" and the space considered "sacred".

Page no.31: "Consumer Edge" highlighting marketing, advertising, media, the changing society - where business meets the customer.

Page no.32: Times Sports, Extra

II. The second pull-out of 12 pages entitled "Bombay Times" included the following:

Page no.1: Film celebs

Page no.2 & 3: Boom town Rap

Page no.4: Leisure

Page no.5: Full page advertisement

Page no.6:Art & Culture

Page no.7:Cyberia that incorporated emerging concepts in computerized areas.

Page no.8: Full page advertisement about films and theatre

Page no.9: Understanding MEN

Page no.10: Body & Soul - 10 tips for better sex and sex related things

Page no.11: Entertainment (mostly semi-nude and topless female models)

Page no.12: Back beat- exciting poses of women and gossip about filmdom.

III. This four page pull-out is captioned "Food Bazar". It deals with wholesale prices, mostly advertisements of item such as grocery that can be purchased at a discount.

IV. The last one is a glossy pull-out of eight pages entitled "Times Property".

The impact on Hindustan Times

It would be wrong to presume that MS. Shobhna Bhartia was not aware of the plot that thickened the pages of her rivals. But she was more confident of the dark horse who maintains constant speed without bothering for acceleration. The Bombay (sorry! Mumbai) edition of HT dataed July 30, 2005 consisted of 36 pages of broadsheet + a 16 page pull-out of tabloid length. The main paper consisted of 24 broadsheets, three pull-outs worth 20 pages and one pull out worth 16 pages of tabloid length. Invitation price being Rs.2/50, the total no. of pages was not mentioned on the front page that displayed micro news at the bottom of 1st column and the resume of inner pages at the end of the last column. The initial five pages (after the front page) were devoted to the city and the disaster it witnessed due to deluge. Page no. seven to 9 captioned, "HT Nation" were full of news items from different parts of the country.

Editorial, leader, a middle by Khuswant Singh and letters to the editor were accommodated on Page no.10. Page no. 11 captioned "Insight" appeared to be reserved for the analysis of current problems. This particular issue was focused on the disaster that engulfed Bombay during those days. Page no.12 was captioned "The Universe and Everything" under which write-ups on the emerging issues in science, medicine and technology were highlighted. Three pages (from page no.13 to 15) were devoted to international news, inter-continental celebs vis a vis diplomatic undercurrents. Page no. 16 was full of stock market news while three pages (page no.17 to 19) captioned "HT Business" were devoted to corporate news. Page no.20 to 22 were captioned "HT Sport" while the 23rd page was a full page advertisement that praised Narcissus. Surprisingly, one more page i.e. the 24th was also devoted to sport.

    I. The first pull-out: It consisted of eight pages as follows:

Page no.1:   A feature on Bharat Shah, Producer No.1/ Page 3 phobia

Page no.2:   Automobiles

Page no.3:   Hollywood (care: not to be confused with Bollywood)

Page no.4:   City diary of movies/T.V. Channels/messages for beloved ones/Zodiac

Page no.5:   Sona bath, beauty tips and

Page no.6:   Party time and pictorial advertisements of movies

Page no.7:   Media news/jingles/gossip about everything regarding life style.

Page no.8:   Glamour - gossip about filmdom.

    II. The second pull-out: A 16 page pull-out of tabloid length devoted to photo coverage of the deluge in Bombay.

III. The third pull-out: HT Estates (4 pages)
IV. The fourth pull-out: HT Comics (4 pages)

A comparative account of coverage is given below:

A Comparative Account of Coverage in DNA, TOI & HT

Dated 30.07.2005

	Items	Name of Journals		
		DNA	**TOI**	**HT**
1	City coverage	08 pages	07 pages	05 pages
2	National news	03 pages	07 pages	03 pages
3	International news	04 pages	05 pages	03 pages
4	Money matters, business, corporate news and share market	08 pages (Pink)	04 pages	04 pages
5	Sports	05 pages	04 pages	04 pages
6	Changing life style	10 + 4 pages	12 pages	08 pages
7	Real estate	08 pages	08 pages	08 pages
8	Comics	NIL	NIL	01 page
9	Media and consumer interaction	01 page	01 Page	01 page
10	Automobiles	NIL	NIL	01 page
11	Hollywood	NIL	NIL	01 page
12	Entertainment guide	01 page	01 page	01 page

It is worth recalling that the Bombay edition of Hindustan Times was launched on 14th of July 2005 while that of DNA on 30th of July in the same year. After one year of cut-throat competition it was revealed that the real competition was between Hindustan Times & DNA and had nothing to do with the Old Lady of Boribunder whose re-sale value in terms of raddi (trash) ensured maximum return even for those who were not acquainted with the English language. What multiplied its weight was a copy of the Mumbai Mirror supplied free with every copy of the Times of India sold in Bombay. What appeared to be free was in fact a marketing strategy as Mr. Sameer Jain extracted additional revenue on Govt.advertisements (private advertisers were smart enough to choose either TOI or MM) inserted in the Mumbai Mirror for which the Times of India had already billed the Govt. -- a fact that either escaped the attention of the Press Council and the I & B Ministry or was a result of connivance by both of them due mainly to its nature of being a sort of hidden subsidy under the name of a package deal! The complimentary copy of Mumbai Mirror not only ensured an edge over the rivals but it was also intended to be a prototype of an afternoon tabloid that would eventually wipe-out MID DAY. Since all the tabloids published in the afternoon and evening lost ground due to round the clock news and views channels, the Times of India Group also launched one of such channels entitled 'Times Now'.

While the Times of India continues to fetch maximum returns on its raddi, nobody has time in Bombay to unfurl 60 plus layers of the old Lady and twenty plus layers of the budding accomplice who has yet to attain puberty. Besides, it is difficult to carry the same in the overcrowded local trains and buses. The beauty of both Hindustan Times and DNA is that both of them can be handled without extra care and without any compromise on the quality of coverage. As regards quantity, they are not as liberal with page three-perverts as the old Lady is. Usually, DNA has three to four or even more pull-outs besides the main paper but the Hindustan Times does not seem to be a competitor for such appendages. It has planned a limited no. of pull-outs commensurate with its Delhi edition. While Mr. Sameer Jain and Mr. Subhas Goel have additional facility to titillate the Freudian muscles of readers on their television channels, Madam Bhartiya appeared to be contented with a pull-out entitled "HT Style" (till December 2006) which had more pages on Fridays and Saturdays to appease the page-three species of Homosapien Indiana. Besides, a luxury magazine entitled 'SPLURGE' on Saturdays and another glossy one entitled 'BRUNCH' on Sundays are also issued with each copy of the Hindustan Times sold in Bombay. Basically, both the glossy magazines are focused on the wining, dining and concubining patterns of the richest exhibitionists (read potential advertisers). The DNA also issues a glossy magazine entitled 'me' free of charge every Sunday. This magazine is devoted to the favorite obsessions of women in general and the cherished empowerment of the privileged ones in particular.

On 14th of July 2006 Hindustan Times celebrated the first anniversary of its Bombay edition. The festive mood was created well in advance with the help of sponsors and event managers. The Mumbai blast in local trains on July 11, 2006 prompted copy cats to highlight slogans such as "Salam Mumbai" that offended the diminishing no. of realists while exalting the ever-increasing no. of sur-realists. The best gift of the anniversary was a subscription offer of Rs.350/- for two years or Rs.195/- for one year. The DNA also offered one year's subscription at Rs.199/-. In other words, any subscriber could get either DNA or HT for less than Rs.17/- every month. This was a counter-strategy to ward-off the effect of the raddi factor offered by the monopolist. Besides, it also had the potential to increase circulation that could ultimately enhance the rates of advertisement.

A Brief Review of HT dated July 14, 2006

The invitation price continued to be Rs.2.50. The main paper consisted of 24 pages in addition to two pull-outs (total 36 pages). The first pull-out entitled "HT Style Weekend" had twelve pages while a special supplement of 20 pages highlighted the achievements of the preceding twelve months. The supplement had full-page advertisements on 7 pages and advertisement material worth three full pages scattered on different pages. By and large, it highlighted major events covered by the HT during the year. Praising Mumbaikars for not retaliating against violence, the first page had an eight column heading:

Indomitable

16 bombs in 3 years. Mumbai is being severely tested. But the hype is true. We won't bow.

The initial six pages described the plight of victims with a good no. of pictures and illustrations followed by full page advertisements on the 7th page. The eighth page had a bold heading 'STOP PRESS' that stated, "for one year Hindustan Times has been part of your journey. Each step has been part of your journey at the road we've travelled together". The remaining pages had glimpses of dreams about the city and condemnation of those who failed to rise to the occasion. In contrast to the 56 pages of the HT priced Rs.2.50, the DNA dated July 14, 2006 had 44 pages priced at Rs.2/-. Since it was HT's anniversary and not that of DNA, it is desirable that a cursory review of DNA's anniversary issue (July 30) is also considered.

A brief review of the Anniversary Day Issue of DNA

In contrast to the usual inscription, the DNA dated July 30, 2006 had an unusual mast, "1 up dna already". This particular issue had 130 pages at its usual price of Rs.2.50. The first page carried a colour picture of Mr. Ratan Tata flanked by the Big 'B' and Mr. Mukesh Ambani. Below the picture was the second lead,

"DNA's 50", Tata, Ambani, Bachchan lead the list

It was a good omen as it signalled an invitation to the mighty ones to join hands for mutual co-operation based on goodwill and corporate advertisements to be reciprocated by image building. Next to this survey was a bold heading that conveyed the editor's thanksgiving to the readers, *"To our Readers, Thanks"*. The opening para reminds of Noah as it stated, "We were born in the wake of a deluge. As we glimpsed the light of day on that drenched dawn a year ago, all we see around us were despair and devastation. We had brought out the newspaper against tight odds, with half our staff unable to make it to work".

Since it was Sunday on July 30, there was no editorial. Unlike other journals the DNA carried its press line as a header till the second week of April 2007. One special feature of the anniversary issue was Readers' Day with DNA in which readers inter-acted with the editorial staff (including the Chief Editor) on various issues of national and international significance. According to the resume published on the same page, "on our first anniversary we invited five readers to meet members of the editorial board for a conversation. The result was a stimulating discussion on several subjects from policy to sports, from coverage of the arts to why criminals are allowed to contest elections". What fascinated me on this page was the following utterance:

"Newspapers have a very clear idea of where they stand on political issues".

In January 2006 DNA launched its financial journal, 'DNA Money' from Indore. Subsequently, the Ahmedabad edition was launched on August 29, 2006. Being aware of these developments, HT also declared the launch of its business newspaper for which it had already entered into an agreement with *The Wall Street Journal.*

In the first week of January 2007 HT re-designed its format. The main paper continued to be of 18 to 20 pages on week days and 24 pages on Sundays followed by a second part entitled "HT2 Business and the World". Page three perverts with potential to emerge as advertisers were bundled into a separate tabloid consisting of 24 pages (12 broadsheets approx.), four pages for the classified ads and need-based pull-outs of 4 pages each for real estate and impact features. The re-structuring was symbolic. It also heralded a message that the HT would not compete in terms of no. of pages or pull-outs as it had already reached its break-even point. Subsequently, the format of the second page was re-designed in November, 2007 and was captioned, 'Hindustan Times Business'.This consisted of eight pages including the classified section, 'Yellow Pages'.

On the first day of February, 2007 HT Media gave another jolt to the DNA by launching its much publicized business daily 'Mint' from New Delhi and Bombay in collaboration with the *Wall Street Journal.* It seems that the Banglore edition was also conceived in February,2007as the same was launched exactly after nine months in November,2007. As stated earlier, DNA had already launched its financial pull-out as an independent business newspaper from Indore and Ahmedabad with an ulterior motive to emerge as a national daily that could compete with Economic Times and Financial Express. The dream was shattered as it would be difficult for DNA to qualify for a partnership compatible with the Wall Street Journal. It was more than a coincidence that the DNA launched its Ahmedabad and Surat editions in November, 2007..

The title 'Mint' without the definite article sounds somewhat incomplete but the days of Queen's English have 'went'. Hence the trouble. Anyway, Mint happens to be the sixth in the list of business dailies after the Economic Times, Business Standard, Financial Express, Hindu Businessline and DNA Money. Since the launch of Mint has further strengthened the business pages of HT, it is desirable to glance through the latest position. Based on the contents of the Sunday edition dated 25.02.2007, the approximate figures have been listed in the following table. For the purpose of calculation of the total no. of broadsheets, tabloid and crown size pages have been rounded-up to the minimum unit of one broadsheet. The table gives a comparative picture of the three English dailies published from Mumbai (who do not claim to be number one). The figures contained in the table are approximate and there is no claim to accuracy whatsoever.

	Name	Total pages	Price	Ad. pages (count)	Ad. Pages (%)	Price / page
1	Indian Express	36	Rs. 3.00	3	8.33	8.33 paise
2	HT	56	Rs. 3.00	20	36	5.35 paise
3	DNA	54	Rs. 2.50	14	26.34	4.62 paise

The dawn of March, 2007 witnessed a significant change on the edit page. The journal abandoned the practice of publishing the names of corporate directors and members of the managerial and editorial teams. This reduced the press line but it continued to be a header till Mr. Gautam Adhikari headed the editorial team. In the present set-up there is no Chief Editor and the incumbent who co-ordinates with the team of sub-editors and reporters is known as co-ordinator, Content Syndication .Ironically, this coordinator reports to a young boy of his son's age group who in turn reports to the Brand Executive. Since journalism is not bureaucracy, the senior most desk-editor is not likely to succeed the coordinator or the young boy masquerading as management guru. If the harsh realities of survival are any indications, there is every possibility that the conventional wisdom may be reduced to a bevy of copy writers.

Keeping in view the unpredictable nature of market forces it is difficult to retain competent journalists in the same organization unless the employer is financially robust and happens to be a humanitarian in his approach as also one who has launched the journal neither to exploit pauper intellectuals nor to facilitate the nexus between politicians and criminals. The financial viability and short-term success of both DNA and the Bombay edition of HT depends upon the extent to which they are willing to be puppets at the hands of politicians and page-three perverts but their long term success depends upon the extent to which they are willing to be conscience keepers, educators and compassionate employers of visionary journalists without resorting to the deplorable technique of carrot and stick. This necessitates the triumph of corporate culture over the conservative norms of Marwari origin. Needless to say that Mr. Subhash Chandra, has already transcended the Marwari norms in favour of the globalised ones. As regards, MS Bhartia, she made her soliloquies public on a private TV Channel when she stated that creativity is measurable.

Without being harsh to MS Bhartia, her statement should be weighed in the light of the following instance:

During 2001, I wanted to place a matrimonial advertisement for my daughter's marriage under the classified category of minimum rates. The most concessional package offered by the Times of India amounted to Rs.2000/- approx. when I divided this amount by the total no. of alphabets of the proposed copy, it emerged that I was required to shell-out Rs.26/- (Rs. Twenty-six) per alphabet. If the advertiser wanted to begin his copy with a tickmark ( ), he was required to pay Rs.200/- (Rs. Two hundred) extra. If newspapers like the TOI and HT are charging a two digit amount for a single alphabet under the classified advertisements, why have they failed to pay at the rate of Rupee one per alphabet to their scribes in general and those below the rank of Chief Editor in particular?

Although Shobhnajee's statement failed to elicit any reaction at the Editors Guild, I congratulate her for the maiden observations regarding the measurement of creativity which may perhaps elevate our intellectual eunuchs to qualify for an orgasm. Meanwhile, she has already launched a tabloid from New Delhi in collaboration with her arch rival. All said and done, this tabloid is intended to be a 'scarecrow' lest Mr. Subhash Chandra launch the Delhi edition of DNA and cuts a niche in the monopolized market of print media, currently estimated in the range of Rs. 5,000/- to Rs.6,000/- crore or more. Perhaps Shobhnajee is not aware that Mr. Subhash Chandra is also a Marwari whose initial struggle for mundane ambitions and subsequent quest for *VIPASHYANA* has transformed him into a compassionate human being for his confidants but a'hard-core' for his rivals and Frankensteins.

A Comparative Review of Language, Contents and Journalese

The impact of DNA's design and layout is already perceptible not only on the pages of HT and TOI, but also on the pages of language publication like the *Inquilab* (Urdu) and *Nai Dunia* (Hindi) published from Bombay and Indore respectively. Since *cre'me de la cre'me* of Indian scribes is associated with DNA, it has already acquired an innovative edge over HT. Although garbed in pontifical language, the editorial contents of HT continue to be 'Politically Correct'. As against this, Mr. Adhikari's editorial observations were more in the form of a running commentary, easily understood by the younger generation. Presently, Mr. Siddharth Bhatia looks after the edit page but the so called management gurus hardly find any timeslot to imbibe the 'syndication' Here is a glimpse of Mr. Bhatia's state of mind:

"So while someone out there thinks that the readers want only good news about successes and gives them a lot of pabulum, others think that they should be preached to. Journalists fall in this trap all the time. They often strategise and think up new ideas to please the 'market',dishing out formulaic confections which are neither too challenging nor offensive to anyone. The powerful are revered, the rest are 'non people' and don't matter...A newspaper is like a department store that offers something for everyone.But it must reflect the zeitgeist, the spirit of the times"

-DNA, November18, 2007

After Mr. Adhikari's exit, Mr .Ayaz Memon emerged as an editorial heavy weight. For all practical purposes, he is the visible face of the editorial department to both the Chairmen and their cronies. of DNA. Basically, Mr. Memon is a sports editor and commentator. What separates him from his counterparts is his holistic perception of the city of Bombay that enables him to command equal leverage in the eyes of rival press barons like Mr. Sameer Jain and Mr. Subhasha Chandra on the one hand and rival politicians like Mr. Bal Thakrey and Mr. Abu Azmi on the other. He edits 'least' in conformity with the maxim "That Government is the best Government which governs the least" While the syndicated edit page of DNA looks superfluous,it is HT that has stolen the show both in terms of academic depth and grey matter. HT has already reduced its no. of pages and pull-outs. With the exception of front page, city pages and the coverage of Maharashtra, most of its pages are teleported from the Delhi edition. For DNA, such an 'economy' is presently a luxury.

Since no newspaper can afford to pay its scribes on a par with marketing executives, it may be constrained to recruit a new team of scribes whose salary pattern is in conformity with what is being offered by its rivals. Once this is accomplished, the rivals would also be relieved of their munificent mask that pretended to offer counter-offers. Under the circumstances, DNA needs an editorial director who is objective about his own mental health and develops a team of competent scribes, equally free from prejudices, psychological complexes and past affiliations. Calling a cliche', a cliché, such an entity cannot be a brand manager of re-cycled condoms being marketed as 'chewing gum' but a human being par excellence who does not turn 'extra polite' before his employers and 'extra-rude' to his juniors. However, such an incumbent should be shrewd enough to adjudicate the hierarchy of sycophants/ interlocutors who obstruct the validity of link between perception and presentation in the editorial premises. Despite the sustained decline in our journalistic ethos, no journal can afford to survive unless its Chief Editor deals directly with the press baron and not through the assistant to the Brand Manager. If Mr. Sameer Jain's model has succeeded with the 'Old Lady', it is due to the antiquity of TOI and not due to ex-Brand Managers of hotel chains and hair- removing creams.

While MS Bhartia continues to hold international summit on leadership qualities, the DNA has a notional satisfaction that it has bagged the IFRA [Asia Media Gold Award] for Newspaper design. Perhaps the sponsors of the Award are not aware of the astronomical amount of money that Mr. Subhasha Chandra and his corporate colleagues have spent as overhead expenses. Media observers are convinced that DNA has seduced history and would continue to do so in the chronology of Mr. Singhania's INDIAN POST and Mr. Sameer Jain's INDEPENDENT unless Mr. Subhash Chandra turns skeptical about the ulterior motives of all concerned.

11 The Emerging Scenario

When the partition of India became inevitable as a pre-requisite to Independence, it was visualized that there would be no burden of Semitic pressure groups after the formation of Pakistan and the nation could proceed ahead as per the democratic aspirations of the majority of God fearing Indians. But those who migrated to Pakistan, visualized the event to be a beginning of prospective partitions of India.

The founding fathers of the Indian Constitution innocently believed that there would be no misuse of unlimited freedom, Fundamental Rights (FRs) and the Directive Principles of State Policy enshrined in the Constitution. Since the Constitution was drafted in a theoretical and ideal situation, members of the Constituent Assembly failed to visualize the following constraints:

(i) the abuse of FRs by fifth columnists;

(ii) the pan-Semitic affinity of those who shared a genetic or religious bond with the Middle East or Europe;

(iii)adult franchise to all citizens irrespective of their academic level and the ability to differentiate between truth and propaganda;

(iv)the psychological constraints and mental health consideration in respect of those who would be contesting
elections;

(v) the vulnerable position of India in the vicinity of the
geo-politically ambitious neighbours and the ubiquitous
presence of Foreign Intelligence Agencies (FIA's) operating in the dubious garb of tribal-welfare, anthropologi-
cal studies, religious groups and NGO's;

(vi)the political ambition of individuals willing to emerge
as international leaders or "Head of a new State" at the
cost of disintegration of the country;

(vii)the lack of military wisdom in the international arena
due to constant justification of the concept of
"Ahimsa"(non-violence);

(viii) the lack of diplomatic initiative in our Foreign Policy.

As a result, we remained blinkered about our own future
for more than four decades thanks to the Forex Reserve
crises of the 1990's that constrained us to read the writing
on the wall. The Fourth Estate could do it well in advance,
had it not been obsessed with self-congratulatory Narcissism and the hypnotizing propaganda of the Cold War. Perhaps the worst would have been over, if the Press could still
distinguish between Financial Reforms and the dazzling
propaganda in the name of Globalization. In an interview
published in the outlook dated October 17, 2005 Mr. Sham
Lal, one of the former editors of the TOI had observed,
"Globalization has made media part of the entertainment
industry. The result is an undesirable shift in the balance of
power from the editor to the marketing manager". Further,
"the trouble with the print media today is neither related to
the competition for a larger share of readership nor the

available share of advertisement, but the lack of realization of the importance to interpret news in a way that will explain to the readers the difficulties before them and put every contentious issue in a wider perspective... But none of our newspaper devotes enough space to these matters. Their recipe for larger circulation is making news coverage more jazzy, giving more and more space to trivia on celebrities in the world of mass entertainment, fashion and sports. The print media in my opinion has failed to fulfil its obligation of educating the public".

It is desirable to understand Mr. Sham Lal's observations in the light of certain critical events:

I. When the Govt. of India approached Israel in August 2006 to vacate the territory of Lebanon, the Indian press failed to enlighten all concerned whether Lebanon had ever asked Pakistan to vacate Gilgit, Baltistan and Hunza which are parts of Indian territory.

II. With regard to the creation of Pakistan and Israel, the press has uniformly failed to remind readers that both are the by-products of World War II. If some nations criticize the creation of Israel how can the same nations justify the creation of Pakistan? If the Islamic world is of the opinion that Israel has no right to exist at the cost of Palestine, how can they justify the existence of Pakistan at the cost of India and its 15% Muslim population?

III. When Pakistan was in the process of acquiring a nuclear bomb, certain journals of non-Indian origin had published a news items to the effect that Israel had approached the then Indian Prime Minister (Mr. Rajeev Gandhi) to facilitate the re-fuelling of Israeli bombers at Porbundar. The Grapewine had it that Rajeev Gandhi not only declined the proposal but also cautioned Zia-ul-Haq, the Pakistani dictator, against such an eventuality.

As usual, the Indian media failed to warn against the dangerous repercussions (that we are facing now) of such an approach.

IV. Dr. B.R.Ambedkar had suggested job reservations in the public sector for certain weaker sections of the Indian society for a period of ten years. When the prescribed period of ten years was over, the Ruling Party perpetuated the provision considering the significance of vote-banks among weaker sections. At this juncture, the Indian press failed to remind all concerned that to perpetuate job reservations on the basis of caste, creed and religion is tantamount to promote incompetence that may ruin the country. Besides, every act of reservation for potential vote banks is a violation of Article 14 of the Indian Constitution because it denies equal opportunity to meritorious candidates.

V. When the military dictator of Pakistan awarded the highest Pakistani award Nishan-E-Pakistan to the then Indian Prime Minister (Mr. Morarjee Desai) the Indian press failed to educate the people about the rationale of such an act. Had it any missing link with respect to the liberation of Bangladesh or the preponed hanging of the Pakistani Premier, Zulfikar Ali Bhutto?

VI. When Foreign Intelligence Agencies (FIAs) were operating in the garb of Christian missionaries in the North-East regions of India (converting tribals with an ulterior motive to control vote banks through clerics and to recruit innocent faces as potential spies), the Indian Press failed to expose the dangerous liaison. The clue given by our own intelligence units proved to be only a tip of the proverbial iceberg. Retaliating the Indian measures, FIA's permanently poisoned the tribes not only against the Indian Army but everything that is Indian. Subsequently, there was a split among ethnic groups on the basis of genetic links with China and the so called religious bond with the West through Christianity. This was a major success for the Chinese Intelligence Agency whose proper-noun-identity is still not known to the CIA. The ethnic split also resulted in the form of a strategic alliance between China and Pakistan who are presently funding insurgency in Assam and the adjoining north-eastern states of India. In this connection, whatever has come to the notice of the people is either due to strategic leaks orchestrated by the foreign media or on account of the books authored by retired army officers who had worked in the North-East. No national newspaper has ever bothered to post a permanent representative in the North-East who may easily inter-act with various ethnic groups the way the Chinese have infiltrated in this or that garb.

VII. It was a British legacy (rooted in the policy of divide and rule) that discriminated against Jains, Buddhists and Sikhs as non-Hindus. The discrimination assumed political dimensions after Independence due to 'vote-bank' considerations. At this juncture, it was the duty of the Indian Press to educate people that these sects were Protestant features of Hinduism. Buddhism was a revolt against the Brahmanical stranglehold , Jainism was a revolt against rituals and superstition while Sikhism was created as a civil defense group to protect Hindus against forceful conversion at the behest of barbarian rulers. Needless to say, our media is still fuelling communal hatred by propagating a separate identity of those who not only belong to the same religion but to a way of life where dissenting view is respected and clerics have no authority to intervene in the personal life of

153

an individual. The propaganda is so strong that anybody who talks of the organic unity of Hindus, Jains, Buddhists and the Sikhs is considered a communalist.

VIII. When communal riots broke-out in the country after the Babri Masjid controversy, the Indian media failed to convince the people that there can be no justification to fight for a public place of worship in the globalized world. As an alternative, the media could have also educated the people that since Babar was born before Ram repeat, since Babar was born before Ram, the disputed land could be handed-over to the Muslims. This would have given some hind sight wisdom to the Leftist historians who still consider Ram to be a mythological character. Perchance, if it is proved that Ram was born before Babar, then the land may be handed-over to the Hindu organizations. Once the antiquity of the original architect is established, the claims of those who built a subsequent structure or destroyed the original one are automatically diluted. In this connection, it is the additional responsibility of the nationalist Press in general and the Urdu Press in particular to convince our Muslim brethren that the Babri Masjid dispute is not a simple matter of Hindu-Muslim conflict. It symbolises humiliation of one of the most ancient civilizations at the hands of savage invaders who had never heard of terms like "human evolution" and "secularism" even in the holiest of the holy language that they revered. Further, they should also be informed that it is high time in human history to reconcile religious fanaticism with democratic values. The way a non-Islamic shrine cannot be built in Mecca or Madina, a shrine of Semitic origin cannot be tolerated at a place which is supposed to be the birth place of a non-Semitic Prophet especially in the circumstances when the victimized country had already given its own land to the descendants of victors/invaders in the form of Pakistan. Besides, the majority community should also be apprised of the fact that idolatry being a tribal practice, must be abandoned by all those who claim to abide by SANATAN DHARMA as there is nothing SANATAN in any idol, icon or such a representative form. If the disputed land is restored to Hindus, they should build a psychiatric-centre for religious fanatics rather than building a temple.

IX. When communal riots broke-out in Gujarat in the wake of the Godhra incident, majority of educated Hindus felt ashamed of it and condemned the killing of innocent people as a crime against humanity. As against this, no Islamic organization condemned the killings of innocent people in Kashmir where the natives have been constrained to leave their ancestral abodes and to live in makeshift camps permanently. The situation necessitates objective education at the Madarsa level irrespective of vote-bank considerations. The electronic media can play a vital role in this connection.

X. A team of reporters belonging to the London-based 'Sunday Times' investigated the drug, Thalidomide which was marketed as a safe drug for pregnant women but there were several cases of women who had given birth to children with deformity perhaps due to this drug. The journal published its findings and fought the case up to the European Court of Human Rights and won. The company agreed to pay compensation to the victims. But the newspaper had to pay a very heavy price for this as it had already spent one million pounds by way of legal expenses.

It is high time for the Indian press barons to introspect if they have taken any sort of such initiative. Leave alone the legal expenses involved in such an expedition, are they paying adequate remuneration to the editorial staff below the rank of Chief Editor and his Man Friday? The above list of examples is simply illustrative and not exhaustive.

The Political Gender

Since the description of an elephant is not the elephant, no media report can be accurate unless it is reviewed with due skepticism. Whatever may be the extended meaning of the term 'secularism' the Western interpretation of the collective behaviour patterns is considered balanced and critical as it originates in the Ox-bridge jargon and exalts democratic aspirations of ethnic minorities at the cost of the territorial integrity of India. In the context of print media, what are vote-bank considerations for a politician, circulation figures are for a press baron although the real subsidy for a newspaper comes through advertisement and not through subscriptions. Since advertisement rates are linked with circulation figures, they can't afford to soar unless the circulation figures allow them to score. Before a newspaper gets patronage of the corporate world, it cajoles the Government for the same which in turn, links the press baron with the hierarchy of the Ruling Party. Thus, the journal manifests its affiliations in general and the political gender in particular. As a result, the coverage of a particular event conveys different messages in different journals.

Besides Left and Right, the Indian Press is also endowed with a gender called 'hermaphrodite' which is more dangerous than the remaining two. It is this third variety that makes a journal more saffron than the 'Organiser' or the 'Panchjanya' whenever the BJP assumes power.

When Tehelka tried to expose Narendra Mody's alleged role in the 2002 post-Godhra riots immediately before the assembly elections in Gujarat during 2007, it failed to impress the Muslims living in Gujarat. Commenting on the Tehelka expose, one Mohammad Yusuf observed, "I watched the programme and wondered why they were showing this before Diwali. They must be planning another riot before the elections" (Outlook, 12 November 2007, page 46).

Explaining the political strategy of the expose in the same issue, Mr. Chandan Mitra observed, "Self-righteous secularists argue: Modi is demon so whatever is said against him is true and if you want proof, you are a communalist neo-Nazi... Nothing justifies the burning alive of 52 *kar sevaks* at Godhra, and the retribution that followed. But just as Delhi recovered from the Congress-supervised anti-Sikh Pogrom of 1984, so much so that Punjab twice elected that party to power in the state, so has Gujarat(sic). This time there is no trace of a communal cloud overhanging the forthcoming elections. The only issue is Gujarat's spectacular economic development despite the devastating earthquake and the shocking riots. It is for the people of Gujarat to judge who are guilty of re-injecting the virus of communalism into the state's policies, who are friends of Muslims and who are their (hidden camera-carrying) enemies."

Since Mr. Chandan Mitra is considered a pro-BJP journo, the breast-beating secularists may take him with buckets of salt which may augment their own blood pressure. It is in this context that they should also consider the anti-salt remedy presented by Mr. Rajdeep Sardesai:

"On the very day that Lalu Yadav Marched to the Prime Minister's, residence demanding Narendra Modi's arrest in the wake of the Tehelka sting expose, a small group of Sikh widow's were protesting at the capitals Jantar-Mantar on the 23rd anniversary of the anti-Sikh riots. One eye on the TV cameras, the other firmly on the Muslim vote, Lalu was making the headlines. The widows were yesterday's story while the 2002 Gujrat riots have become a cause celebre for the secular establishment, 1984 has never quite acquired the same profile".

- HT, 9th of November 2007

Elaborating his statement, Mr. Sardesai further observed that the anti-Sikh riots were far more horrible than the post-Godhra violence. More than 2,700 people were killed in 1984 riots as per the official death toll; in Gujrat it was a little over a thousand. The 1984 riots have seen 13 convictions; in Gujrat, the fast-track courts have already convicts more than 15 persons in different cases. Rajiv Gandhi's statement that "when a big tree falls, the earth shakes" is regarded history; Narendra Modi's "action-reaction" comment was officially denied. Finally, Sardesai has stressed, "Why then is Modi such a hate figure today for the secularists while Rajiv Gandhi, the then Home Minister, Narsimha Rao and the entire top congress leadership have escaped public censure? The answer might unlock not just the Modi enigma, but also the content of Indian secularism and perhaps indicate just how much India has changed in the last two decades. Modi says in public what many may say in private. A centuries-old, unsaid prejudice that still has not been properly confronted and cauterized is Modi's secret weapon. It makes him more electable. And also more feared".

158

Despite Mr. Sardesai's hint, nothing explains the secret of Mody's spectacular victory during the last two assembly elections despite a sustained media campaign focused at demonising him for right or wrong reasons. Incidentally, I may clarify that the purpose of quoting Mohammed Yunus along with eminent journalists is not aimed at promoting Mody's image. The Point at issue is the Press and its coverage. Since Mody emerged victorious in the last elections despite media campaign against him, the Press should introspect why it failed to report the true feelings of the people who never considered him a demon. Had they considered so, they would not have allowed him to continue as their Chief Minister. Despite that if there was anything 'demonic' in his personality cult, it was a reflection of popular sentiments. The moral of the story is that people wanted to befriend a demon who could help them against other demonic species. In other words, the demon rules the heart of people and the Fourth Estate was perhaps over enthusiastic to deprive the people of their right to security against threat perception? For any reason if it was the bounden duty of the Press to do so, it is still not too late to introspect as to why the same Press is silent about its own nexus with the politicians and criminals? What prevents it from exposing the anti-national elements in Jammu and Kashmir? Why the Press has failed to investigate the reasons of the spurt in crime rate? Why the act of kidnapping has emerged as a sunrise industry? Why our borders are porous despite the presence of BSF? And the list of "Whys" is not exhaustive.

Islamic Terror and the Press

It is high time for the Indian Press to expose the pretensions of secular hypocrisy implied in slogans such as *Majhab Nahi Sikhata, aapas mein bair rakhna*. Even if we don't take into consideration the torching of the Sabarmati Express in Godhra and the incineration of over 53 women and children at one go and the bombing of the Akshardham Temple in Ahmedabad, it is difficult to forget the following acts of terrorism: On 8 August, 1993 there was a bomb blast at the RSS office in Chennai killing eleven and injuring seven. On 14 February, 1998 there was a serial car bombing in Coimbatore killing 46 and injuring over 200. In May-June 2000 there was a series of 13 bomb blasts in churches in Andhra Pradesh, Karnataka and Goa, killing nearly 50. The Indian Institute of Science, Bangalore was attacked on 28 December 2005 by an L-e-T backed group. Again, on 18 May 2007 the Lashkar-e-Toiba arranged a blast at the Mecca Masjid in Hyderabad, killing 16 persons. Besides, the Raghunath Temple in Delhi and the Sankat Vimochan at Varanasi were also attacked during 2006. According to the Anti-Terrorist Squad, ISI sponsored groups like the L-e-T and Al Badr have both active and sleeping modules in India. Meanwhile, the Outlook magazine had pointed out that there was a sizeable educated Muslim population who are now seen as likely candidates for jihadi indoctrination.

As against the above chronology of disaster, our official position remained quite different and the politically correct statement made at the National Press Club in Washington during 2006, ran as follows, "We have 150 million citizens who practice the faith of Islam. And I say it with some pride, that not one of them has joined the ranks of these gangs like the Al Qaida or other terrorist outfits..."

If the targeted vote bank is still not impressed, here is another reminder to all concerned: When Al-Zawahiri reappeared on our television screens to urge all Muslims to join the Jihad to destroy the West , our own leaders were losing sleep over Muslims being "labelled" as also after seeing the face of the mother of the alleged bombers from Banglore.

Unfortunately, our political leadership never lost sleep for the victims of train blasts in Bombay despite the pale faces of two hundred mothers who lost their innocent children for no fault of theirs. This was the time when the Indian Press could boycott the person concerned for a good cause. Pallbearers of Democracy ! Are you listening?

Blogs and Bloggers

In the present scenario there has been a constant decline in the circulation of newspapers throughout the affluent world. According to reports published in the Economist during the last week of August 2006, circulation had been falling in America, Western Europe, Latin America, Australia and New Zealand for decades. In the past few years websites have hastened the process of this decline. In Switzerland and the Netherlands newspapers have lost half their classified advertisements to the internet. In the same report it was also predicted that over the next few decades half the rich world's general papers may have to fold up. According to the Newspaper Association of America, the number of people employed in the industry fell by 18 per cent between 1990 and 2004. Shares of listed newspaper firms have also registered a decline. The share price of The New York Times Company had fallen by 50 per cent during the last four years or so. In 2005, Knight Rider, the company that owned several American dailies was constrained to sell its pulpdom. It had 18000 employees, 32 daily newspapers with a combined circulation of 3.7 million. The company sold itself to the MeClatchy Company for $ 4.5 billion and the assumption of $ 2 billion in debts. Thus, a media company with relatively high profit margins disappeared for good. In India, the case is different. Despite Internet, newspapers have registered an increase in circulation. The largest circulated English daily is published not from London or Washington DC but from 7 Bahadur Shah Zafar Marg, New Delhi.

Consequent on the advent of blogs, a debate has started on the survival of conventional media. According to a rough estimate, there are one hundred million blogs in the cyberspace out of which one lakh have originated in India. According to Peter Griffin, blogger and copywriter, a blog called "South East Asia Earthquake and Tsunami" that he had started in December 2004, received more than a million visitors. Of late, Scott Carney, an American freelancer has taken initiative to enlist the support of bloggers for journalism. If he succeeds, many more journalists may lose their jobs in due course of time.

Commenting on the scenario, the DNA in its editorial (September 13, 2006) had observed, "Blogs are for the most part, instant outbursts of views and opinion and occasionally, first hand reportage by untrained writers who may be eye-witnesses to an incident. But bloggers lack the rigour of fact-checking and do not have the built-in filters of newspapers to ensure that anything that is printed passes the litmus test of being accurate, objective, balanced and non-libellous".

Subsequently, in an edit page article captioned, "Will blog kill the print star" (DNA dated September 17, 2006) Mr.

Pradyuman Maheshwari observed, "yes, not all bloggers observe the discipline of ascertaining facts. This is possible because they think they know it all or it could be plain carelessness. But does this not also hold true for the media the masses trust - newspapers, magazines and television channels? There may be senior journos in publications who sift through stories and knick out stuff that appears biased, but which Indian papers - national dailies included - have full time fact-checkers and researchers to double check every thing? Unidentified sources are hence often used in newspapers and one is supposed to assume it is correct...very few organizations strictly observe a code of conduct or have an ombudsperson ...it is ludicrous to rubbish blogs (and bloggers) as immature".

Since Mr. Maheshwari was a junior member of the editorial team headed by Mr. Gautam Adhikari, it appears that the contradiction was not due to lack of co-ordinations between the editor and his team but a managerial strategy to humiliate the editor for a desired result. Brand Managers, are you listening?

According to Philip Knightley "Those newspapers which survive do so by slashing editorial staff to the bone and spending the money saved on promotion, the success of which can be measured". Rupert Murdoch had once commented "Never give journalists a budget. If you do, the bastards will spend the lot". Accordingly, he introduced the concept of "Zero budgeting" under which journalists have to justify to an accountant the expenses of the assignment they are about to undertake. Some newspapers now even keep files at analyzing journalists' performance- how much did they spend on an assignment divided by how many words finally appeared in the paper. The answer could later influence which journalist was sent on a story, a five-cents-a word reporter being more likely to go than a twenty-cents-a word one. The quality of words is irrelevant.[24]

---

[24] Outlook, October 17, 2005

12 Addressed to Mr. Editor

All around me I saw mediocre editors flourishing. They possessed minuscule professional competence but were extremely adept at intra-office intrigue and the felling of competitors. Readers may think that since I do not command any editorial position, I am blaming those who have reached the top. In all fairness to journalistic ethics, I must clarify that the above observation is not mine and has been extracted from Mr. Vinod Mehta's Book, *Mr. Editor, how close are you to the PM?*

In the same volume Mr. Mehta has cornered our editors as follows:

"Indian editors especially, have a tremendous fondness for entertaining and being entertained by the high and the mighty. Lunches, dinners, tea parties with Ministers and Prime Ministers are coveted as badges of honour. A politician will reciprocate by remembering your wife's first name or your son's birthday. A cake, even some flowers may arrive. Alas, such conviviality carries with it one of the great dilemmas of political writing. "How do you write objectively about your friends? How do you dine with them and dine on them later?"

Since the majority of our 'competent' editors have maintained a studied silence on Mr. Mehta's observations, perhaps, it is desirable not only to differentiate between 'chalk and cheese' but also to identify the silver lining in the light of the following categories of our editorial fraternity.

I. **Conventional Moralists** like Devdas Gandhi, Frank Moraes, Pothen Joseph, Nanporia, Sham Lal, S. Mulgaonkar, S.Nihal Singh, Hiranyamay Karlekar and their intellectual off springs. The list is not exhaustive but only illustrative.

II. **Trust-ridden Editors** like the late Chelapti Rao of National Herald, Mr. Hari Jaisingh of Tribune, Mr. Shekhar Gupta of Indian Express and Mr. Chandan Mitra of Pioneer who worked/are still working on behalf of some public or private trust/an organization of journalistic origin as its managing trustee or a trustee-cum-editor/ director-cum-editor without being an editorial director.

III. **Aboriginal Editors or their Men Friday masquerading as editors** With a very few exceptions like the late Sadanand of FPJ, Mr. Aveek Sarkar of The Telegraph, Mr. C.R.Irani of The Statesman and Mr. N.Ram of the Hindu, this category includes proprietor-editors and their mannequins like the "post-Girilal Jain" generation of editors who pretended to edit the vital statistics of the Old Lady of Boribunder. Again, this category is not exhaustive but ubiquitous if not universal.

IV. **The Hype and Hoopla variety** of go-go guys that includes Mr. Khushwant Singh, Mr. Priteesh Nandy, Mr. M.J.Akbar, Mr. Veer Sanghvi, and late Mr. R.K.Karanja of Blitz fame. The obsession of these editors with Narcissus can hardly be over-emphasized.

V. **'They Also Ran' variety** that includes answers to questions such as who is the editor of Free Press Journal? or of the Bombay edition of 'The Asian Age'.

VI. **Eunuchs in the harem variety** this includes management crooks who cannot perform the act but shamelessly pretend to guide those who are biologically equipped to do so. With a very few exceptions like the factotums engaged by Mr. Sameer Jain, this category continues to remind the validity of 'Peter Principle.'

VII. **The clean slate variety** editors who have not allowed their conscience to be conditioned by any ethnic, religious or political ideology may be included under this category. Beginning with the late Behram Contractor, the list may be further stretched to include Pronoya Roy, Vinod Mehta, Rajdeep Sardesai Barkha Dutt and a few Hindi Journalists like Rahul Barpute, Rajendra Mathur (since deceased) and the "Post Roopkanvar Avtar" of Mr. Prabhash Joshi. While Rajendra Mathur and Prabhash Joshi emerged as representatives of the first elite generation of Hindi journalists, those initiated by the duo continue to be half-baked and obsessed with their own brand of inferiority complex.

More often than not, it is the H&H (Hype and Hoopla) variety that has apologized in private for what it exposed in public! How else one reconciles with Mr. Khushwant Singh's self-proclaimed atheism when he returned all the national honours in the wake of Operation Blue Star? When General Pervez Musharraf took military action against the inmates of the Lal Masjid of Lahore (July 2007) the same Khushwant Singh wrote in this syndicated column (HT 21.07.2007), "When religious practices come into conflict with laws of the state, the latter must prevail. Heads of religious organizations tend to become self-willed and arrogant. They must be cut to size when they cross the limits". Similarly, it became increasingly difficult to justify the secular credentials of Mr. Priteesh Nandy when he was elected to the Rajya Sabha on the strength of the Shiv Sena. How do we reconcile with Mr. M.J.Akbar's unique position as editor of two English dailies (Deccan Chronicle along with Asian Age is owned by a Saudi Arabian Company with editorial leadership under Mr. M.J.Akbar) despite his failure to have sustained the publication of an established tabloid like Blitz when it was taken-over by Mr. Vijay Mallya? By the way, have you ever seen Mr. Veer Sanghvi on a TV screen interviewing a semi-nude celebrity who elaborates the recipe of mushrooms that may or may not augment the sperm count of defunct editors? And again, by the way, who should write an edit-page article on the pitfalls of Indian Foreign Policy resulting in Mr. Shashi Tharoor's defeat for the top post at the United Nations? Should it be attempted by the nude celebrity introduced by Mr. Editor?

Speaking on the occasion of receiving the International Press Institute (IPI) Award on behalf of 'Outlook' in December 2007, Mr. Vinod Mehta emphasized the following points.

I. Journalists should head readers not get led by them.

II. Brand Managers with honourable exceptions are congenitally incapable of understanding the nature and purpose of journalism. They simply cannot understand it by virtue of their background: which is sales in order to maximize profits. They can never understand that content is more than what readers want.

III. As against the projected dictum, "the reader is king", Mr. Mehta has raised the following questions:

(i) if some readers or viewers wish to see or read about pedophelia should we oblige?

(ii) if some readers or viewers wish to see or read about wife beatings, should we oblige?

(iii)Research shows that most readers desire to read more international news yet the international pages of a paper are the least read. International news may be good for the soul but it does nothing for the circulation.

(iv)Readers insist that the price of their morning paper does not matter. It is such a vital part of their life that they would happily pay the extra rupee for it. Yet, as Rupert Murdoch and Sameer Jain have demonstrated, print publications are extremely price sensitive. You can bleed the opposition by cover price cuts. The phrase, "invitation price" terrifies rival publishers.

(v) Readers will tell you that they want a single section, compact morning paper. They don't want sections and supplements dropping out. Yet the opposite is true. Papers with multi-sections prosper, others suffer.

VI. Editors in India are endangered species, but only a good and professional editorial team can decide what is news and what is humbug.

While no editor with a vertebral column would disagree with Mr. Mehta there are certain other aspects about which an overwhelming majority of our editors (aboriginal ones included) are hardly aware:

(i) While they are gladly willing to be sodomized by the Western authors like Mr. Coleridge (the author of 'Paper Tigers'), they are always, busy with some cute excuse when an Indian author seeks an appointment. Accordingly, it is easy to get an appointment with a Chief Minister rather than with Mr. Samir Jain in Bombay or with Mr. Aveek Sarkar in Calcutta (sorry! Kolkata). Perhaps Mr. Dileep Padgaonkar was right when he maintained that he was doing the most important work next only to the Prime Minister of India. Perhaps, he may be doing the same thing even now but for the "Prime Minister in waiting".

(ii) When any creative work/book is addressed to the editor by any author for review, he never receives any reply. Either the book is retained in the reference section/library of the journal or sold in *raddi* in due course. The author continues to be clueless despite repeated reminders. Notable exceptions being works supposedly written by politicians/bureaucrats or their factotums /paramours. More often than not, our editors are not aware that a creative writer has an edge over the so called editor who plagiarises in the name of journalism with phrases such as, "On the one hand.......while on the other." It is desirable that the publication with intended review should be acknowledged and if it is not possible to publish a review, the same should be returned. As an alternative, it may be clarified on the edit page, "Please do not send books for review". If there are certain "service charges" the same should be conveyed to the author.

(iii)When it comes to corporate communication in areas other than advertising and circulation, the majority of our editors/ managing editors/brand managers prefer to remain silent even when they are approached through a registered letter. The studied silence is not specific to any person or organization but it is a regular practice even when they are approached by govt. officials under statutory requirements. The most glaring precedent concerns the Bhabosh Dutta Committee constituted by the Government of India to examine newspaper economics. While certain journals did cooperate with the Committee after repeated reminders, certain others (including the 'Journalists' Journal) preferred to remain silent.

Mr. Chanchal Sarkar, the Founding Director of the Press Institute of India had one observed, "The media, individually and collectively, give precious little information about themselves despite this being an information age with a superhighway spreading to the horizon... The jagged question, therefore, is how to have liberalization with responsibility, liberalization for the benefit of Indian Citizens. As I have said there is very little thinking on this by media professionals and governments. Owners are interested in profits, not responsibility... What we seem to want is a sensation of intellect without the discomfort of thought."[25]

Readers may think that Mr. Chanchal Sarkar's observations regarding corporate communication on the part of media were perhaps true ten years ago when brand executives were confined to the marketing of bustline-developers and re-cycled condoms. Now that management gurus with specialization in communication, motivation and leadership style are at the helm of affairs, the position may be somewhat better! Not really. As an example, I am submitting a

---

[25] Mainstream, March 29, 1997.

case study that I undertook in 2007. In short, a common friend recommended my name to a press baron for the post of Chief Editor. The press baron in turn, phoned me to contact his brand manager on a pre-determined date. After confirmation of the appointment in advance, I reached the premises half an hour before time. The executive was late by one hour. He called me after ten minutes, perused my papers for five minutes or so and then talked to me for about ten minutes. At the end, he confessed that he knew nothing about journalism and that I should talk to his deputy. To my surprise, the deputy was not available in the office although the appointment was fixed well in advance. When the deputy was contacted over the cell phone, he reached the office after half an hour. We talked for a few minutes, and he obliged me with his visiting card for further inter-action. When I failed to receive any communication for a month, I wrote back to the Press baron about the inter-action with his brand manager and the subsequent deadlock. This was followed by a diplomatic reply to the effect that depending upon a vacancy in future, I would be informed suitably.

I was aware that the brand manager was not reporting to the press baron but to one of his partners designated as the Managing Director. Subsequent investigations revealed that the brand manager never reported the matter to his boss.

In hindsight, one may visualize two possibilities: the press baron was diplomatic enough who never intended to consider my bio-data but was not in a position to say 'no' to my friend's proposal. Secondly, he might have been studying the modus operandi of his brand manager vis-a-vis an intruder.

To my mind, there was a distinct third possibility concerning the caliber of all concerned. Without asking me to see his brand manager, the press baron could tell my friend what was conveyed to me after one month. As an alternative, he should have invited me in his chamber to convey what was conveyed through his lethargic hierarchy after a month. All said and done, it was a theatrical version of public sector scenario where the *dramatis personae* were more deplorable than their bureaucratic counterparts. I can only pity the press baron and his so called experts.

In the globalized economy almost every newspaper/financial journal/magazine has published details of emoluments and perks payable to head honchos and professionals in different industries. Surprisingly, no editor worth his salt has ever bothered to publish an article or impact feature focused on the figures of salary package being offered to the top ten editors of the country, to say nothing about the comparative position *vis-a-vis* the electronic media. Majority of journalists of a multi-edition daily are not aware that their salary package is hardly comparable with the one being offered to some copy writers of eminent ad-agencies. Besides, the advertising tariff in a journal that claims to sell 10 lakh copies or more is Rs.50/- per alphabet or so. As against this, our editors/columnists are getting peanuts for what they write in terms of columns or stories. It is high time that the remunerations offered to the editorial staff is rationalized vis-a-vis the rates charged for classified ads. If the ad rate is Rs.50/- per alphabet, the journalist should also get at least Re.1/- per alphabet. If the confusion is due to 'per column centimeter', the scribes may also be paid at the rate of per column centimeter. During early 1990s, Mr. Shekhar Gupta was the highest paid Chief Editor- cum-CEO

(Rs.1.75 lakh p.m.) and Mr. Mani Shankar Aiyer was the highest paid columnist (Rs.10,000 per article). Keeping in view the inflationary trends in the second fastest growing economy of the world, and the ever-increasing advertisement tariffs imposed by the newspapers, there should have been a judicious revision of wages payable to the scribes. While the mainstream English press has shrunk during the last ten years, there has been a mushroom growth of multi-edition language dailies claiming to publish ten to thirty editions but their editors' salary package is still not comparable with the one paid to Mr. Shekhar Gupta 17 years ago.

According to management gurus, salary package in the corporate world depends upon the following factors:

   (i) Employee's performance
   (ii) Employer's corporate performance
   (iii)The prevailing rate of inflation
   (iv)Prevailing trends in the Industry.
   (v) Demand-supply gap in terms of availability of skilled staff.
   (vi)The cost of living (city specific).

When Mr. Abhaya Chhajlani was President of the Indian Newspaper Society, he had vehemently maintained that there was no justification of a Wage Board for working journalists. As against this, there has been a constant hike in salaries in the Indian Corporate Sector (other than print media where it was occasional). On an average, salaries in the corporate sector in India grew by 15.1% during 2007. However, this does not include Realty and Infrastructure sectors where the hike was 25.2 %. Since the Realty Sector cannot survive without advertising, it is constrained to share its profit with the print media by way of expensive ad-campaigns. Perhaps it is desirable that while publishing ownership details in the first week of March, press barons also declare the total no. of editorial staff and the percentage of staff-strength facilitated with a hike in salary.

What gives an 'edge' to brand managers over editors is the editorial ignorance about the cost of blank broadsheets and the mechanism implied in value addition. Every press baron who sells 40 pages (20 broadsheets) plus supplements for Rs.2/- or Rs.1.50/- is aware that the cost of 20 blank sheets is more than that of the newspaper. If this is so, how does the brand manager manage the gap? Here is an illustration by Mr. Ravindra Kumar of the Statesman who has taken pains to calculate the per kilogram worth of two English dailies published from New Delhi:

"The cumulative circulation of the two largest English Newspapers grew in the city by 116 per cent between June 1993 and December 1998... If these figures are accurate, and conventional logic would argue they must be because they were certified by ABC, there must have been a massive change in the social characteristics of New Delhi and parts of northern India serviced by these newspapers. There must have been a huge increase in the literacy levels of the populace. We wouldn't just be talking about functional literacy as characterized by the government's literacy programmes, but a growth in literacy levels among the segment that reads English newspapers. Sometime in 1993-94, the cover price of New Delhi's two biggest English newspapers was reduced to Rs.1.50/-. At the same time, the commission payable to hawkers rose to about 38 per cent of the cover price. As per ABC requirements, the circulation figures could be considered 'Net Paid Sale' only if the publisher showed return of 93 paise per copy in his books.

Their minimum daily page-level was between 28 and 32 while occasionally, it could be as high as 48 and 52.

When weighed, it was revealed that 6.17 copies of a 28 page newspaper is equivalent to one kilogram. As regards a 32 page newspaper, it is 5.40 copies weighed one kilogram. To qualify as Net-Paid-Sale, the return from 6.17 copies would have to be Rs.5.40 (6.17 x .093) and from 5.40 copies it would have to be Rs.5.02 (5.40 x .93).

In other words, if a newspaper vendor could dispose of the papers he bought from the publisher to a waste paper dealer at Rs.5.40 a kg in the first case, and Rs.5.02 a kg in the second, he would not have to suffer the inconvenience of cycling his way through the crowded, pollution-choked by-lanes of New Delhi... Whether newspapers were actually sold as waste is something only the vendor and the waste paper dealer can answer. We can only look at the probability of such an occurrence.

In early 1994, the price of waste paper was about Rs. 5.40 per kg. By May 1995, it had gone up to Rs.7.41. In August 1995, waste sold at 6.90. It remained around this figure until May 1996 when the price rose to 7.65. For the next two years, the price moved up and down, but never below Rs. 5.46.

Thus, in May 1996, if a newspaper vendor purchased copies of a 52 page newspaper worth Rs.1000/- he would have been able to immediately realise Rs.2,470/- by selling it to a waste paper dealer. Had he instead taken the trouble to sell it to readers, he would have realised Rs.1,612/-.... The evidence is strong but circumstantial.

Since an intellectual employed as editor may not be adept at the art of recycling newspapers as *raddi*, and since ad-tariffs cannot be raised without a significant graph of circulation figures, the editor is condemned to remain a liability till he is willing to be initiated in the dubious art of mask-management for pulp-whores, power-pimps, management-crooks and *ex-officio* intellectuals.

The way eunuchs pretend to be feminine, the Indian Print media in general and the electronic one in particular has projected a 'Leftist gender' against the stark reality of its 'Rightist' patterns of ownership. This not only reflects an error of perception but has also resulted in the form of undue publicity to *agents provocateurs* and fifth columnists masquerading as social workers and journos.

Epilogue

Saline water being spermicidal
the mirror failed to conceive my tears .
Being pregnant with past images
obstructed remained the present vision.

Then they called a glass expert
from Belgium or Paris
who proposed to abort
images, unwilling to distort.

Separating the fram
the expert suggested amnesia
followed by a split therapy
that caused a hair in the mirror.

Distortion being short of abortion
what emerged was a transition
of collage, a blurred vision
that delivered a schizo mirror.

Promoting further splits
splitting mirrors facilitate
manic depression, bi-polar illness
mitosis, meiosis, this or that psychosis.

Deveriya is a Bombay based poet, linguist and media observer with highly acclaimed works in the realm of psycho-analysis. In the present volume, he has traced the origin of the nexus between politicians and press barons on the one hand and between criminals and the "duo" on the other. Obviously, such an exposé would not have been possible without prolonged inter-action with the dramatis personae and a constant verification of the "trash" projected as news in the media. Besides, he has critically examined the process of Indianization of the Fourth Estate. The book is not only useful for journalists, politicians and press barons but also for mafia dons planning 'diversification'.

Rashid Khosravi
B.Sc. LL.B.
ADVOCATE,
Bombay High Court